Great
Myths
of
Economics

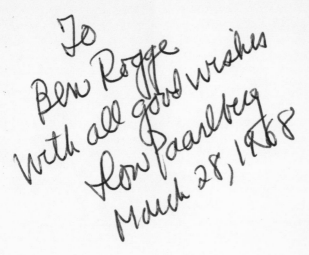

To
Ben Rogge
with all good wishes
Don Paarlberg
March 28, 1968

GREAT
MYTHS
OF
ECONOMICS

by DON PAARLBERG

THE NEW AMERICAN LIBRARY

This book is dedicated
to the fine teachers who made economics
come alive for me, teachers to whom I owe the excitement
of a great learning experience. Among the best
were Professors J. A. Estey and E. C. Young
of Purdue and Professors F. A. Pearson and
H. L. Reed of Cornell.

First Printing

Published by The New American Library, Inc.
1301 Avenue of the Americas, New York, New York 10019
Published simultaneously in Canada
by General Publishing Company Ltd.
Library of Congress Catalog Card Number: 68–16213
Printed in the United States of America

Preface

"Rain before seven, dry before eleven," the old-timer would say, scanning the sky on a rainy morning. Looking at a bright sunset, the sea captain would recall the old saying, "Red at night, sailor's delight," and expect good weather the next day. "Feed a cold and starve a fever" was an honored prescription for many years. I knew a man who carried a potato in his pocket to cure his rheumatism, another who ate fish in the belief that it stimulated his brain, and another who would undertake no new venture on a Friday. There is widespread belief in a number of historical tales, including George Washington's assault on the cherry tree and Lincoln's five-mile walk to return an overpayment of three cents.

These beliefs are a combination of half-truth, myth, folklore, superstition, and outright fiction. Yet it would be an error to dismiss them as being without significance. They have at least some fragmentary factual basis and a degree of plausibility. If it rains before seven it is quite likely to stop before eleven; most rains continue for less than four hours. If one believes that Friday is a bad day to start a project he is unlikely to commit himself enthusiastically to it and if he does, the chances for success will probably be less than average. Washington's veracity and Lincoln's honesty were indeed attributes of these two men, though overstated in the mentioned legends.

Even if a myth has only a flimsy factual basis it may well be worth study, because one's belief tells us something quite important about him. It tells us what he wants to believe, it predicts his behavior at least in part, and it identifies the erroneous ideas that will have to be eradicated if valid ones are to take their place.

Myths are by no means confined to the weather, home remedies, or to history. The social studies have their full share. "Mythology," said President Kennedy, "distracts us everywhere — in government as in business, in politics as in economics, in foreign affairs as in domestic policy."

Recently there has been an effort to demythologize several areas of study, notably history and theology. This book pushes the movement into economics. Aware of the vagueness of the line between myth and reality, I know that I have set myself a difficult task. And, having heard the anguished cries of those whose deep convictions have been labeled myths, I am aware that I may stir up considerable protest. It has been suggested to me that it would be better to build on top of the old myths, as the Egyptians build new mud huts on the mounds left from their ancestors' homes. Nevertheless, the effort here is to thrust the old myths aside and build from as firm a foundation as possible.

It is not surprising that economic myths are widespread. Economics did not emerge as a distinct body of thought until the eighteenth century; indeed, it is still struggling to become an acknowledged science. John Maynard Keynes, the English economist, said a generation ago that economists had not yet earned the right to be listened to attentively. Gardner Ackley, Chairman of the Council of Economic Advisers, recently characterized economic understanding as being in a pre-Newtonian state. The Joint Council on Economic Education estimates that only 3 percent of those eligible to vote in the United States have had as much as one formal course in economics. Imagine the mathematical competence of the population if only 3 percent of us had ever studied arithmetic!

Furthermore, economics is beset with jargon that makes it difficult to understand, even for the diligent scholar. Someone has said that economics is the science of stating the obvious in terms of the incomprehensible.

Economic folklore is a powerful force in public policy. In a country with representative government, the beliefs and attitudes of the voting public are the ultimate criterion for action. If beliefs are based to a large degree on mythology, political demands will reflect these myths. Elected officials, however wise, will find political pressures hard to resist. As a direct result of economic mythology, the people may saddle themselves with programs that are in conflict with their true objectives. In the hope of reaching some attractive but unattainable objective, central command may be substituted for individual voluntary action, resulting in the loss of freedom. Likewise, government action that might be helpful to our free society must sometimes be foregone because folklore forbids it. Thus, through both overuse and underuse of government, without our wanting it to happen and perhaps without our even being aware of it, our freedom can be impaired.

The objective of this book is to improve the economic understanding of the general public. The approach is through identifying major myths and half-truths, sorting out what validity they have, pointing out their fallacies, and then setting forth the relevant theory, as generally agreed upon by reputable economists. My belief is that there exists a sufficiently large body of accepted economic theory to provide the basis for a workable free society.

This book differs from most other economics books in several important ways. The differences here cited are not intended to reflect credit or discredit on this book or any other. They are set forth so that the reader will not waste his time searching for something he is unlikely to find.

The book is written for informal reading by people who take no regular courses in economics, as reference reading by persons taking adult education courses, or as supplemental reading by high school and university students. It is not a textbook. Most other economics books are written as texts, for regular classroom study.

The book assumes that the reader is not interested in becoming a professional economist. Most other beginning economics books are written so that they could be the first step toward entry into the profession.

This book attempts to eradicate existing myths, thereby preparing the ground for the seed it then sows. Most economics books make no frontal assault on erroneous belief and undertake no preparation of a seed bed. In effect, they scatter seed on the ground at hand, cloddy, weedy, unreceptive, or well prepared, as the case may be.

Most economics books deal with abstract ideas in theoretical form; this one is primarily concerned with applications. This is the difference between a museum of natural history, where the animals are dead and stuffed, and the open country, where wildlife is found in its native state.

Most writers of economics textbooks try, with varying degrees of success, to avoid commitment regarding the ideological issues of the day. This book frankly treats the market economy, intelligently operated, as a good institution, worthy of serving as the basis for economic life.

Most beginning economics books are comprehensive, covering every important phase of the discipline, and running to as many as a thousand pages. When I told one of my associates that I was writing a manuscript on economic myths, there came the instant reply: "That will be a work in five volumes!" And indeed it might be, were one to treat the subject fully. Such is not my intent. Instead, I concentrate on a limited number of myths. Selected for what reason? Because of their prominence? Their uniqueness? Their aesthetic appeal? For all of these reasons, to some degree. But primarily because these particular myths impose the greatest obstacles to wise economic policy.

This book was conceived during 1958–1961, when I was economic adviser to President Eisenhower. I was impressed with the generally low level of economic literacy in the country and with the handicaps thereby imposed on legislative and administrative processes. I was also impressed with the willingness of many economists to occupy themselves with esoteric refinement of the discipline rather than with the eradication of gross misconceptions. I listed "Seven Economic Fallacies," drawing subconsciously, perhaps, on the idea of the Seven Deadly Sins. For five years, perhaps a proper gestation period for a book of this kind, the list was in and out of the drawer, the subject of intermittent reading and reflection. In the opening half of the book, the fallacies get a chapter each.

If the first half of the book should prove successful, the battlefield will be strewn with myths, dead and wounded. In modern warfare the victor extends aid. In that spirit I offer the second half, an effort at reconstruction.

In these later chapters I shall present, in very brief form, what I believe to be the central economic ideas, the minimum essentials, economics for the layman. These principles are accepted by most Western economists and are not often challenged professionally. Since the ideas I shall present are seldom disputed by economists, they ordinarily receive less attention than is properly their due.

If one understands the elementary ideas set forth in the last half of the book, he should have a basic comprehension of perhaps three-fourths of the economic activity that surrounds him (although not three-fourths of the disputes of professional economists, or three-fourths of economic literature!). Let me add quickly that even this degree of comprehension will not come alone from a single reading — or even many readings — of these chapters. Reflection and other readings are recommended; a list of references will be found in the Appendix. These chapters are offered out of the conviction that in economic theory, as with the English language, to be functionally literate is better than to be illiterate, even though one may not be able to understand or appreciate the most advanced work. Indeed, to move a number of people out of economic mythology into the beginning stages of comprehension may constitute a better deed than to add some increment of professional competence to those already learned.

There have been previous efforts to condense economic principles down to some irreducible minimum. Frank Knight of the University of Chicago used to say that it should be possible to distill economic principles to a single page. Milton Friedman, President of the American Economic Association, contends that the core of the discipline can be stated in five words: "There is no free lunch." Thus I feel some justification for my effort to compress the subject into nine short chapters.

Don Paarlberg
Hillenbrand Professor
Purdue University
1967

Acknowledgment

The souls first encountered by Dante
on his journey through Hell were the spirits of those
who, when confronted with moral crisis,
simply suspended judgment.

This book was assisted financially by
the Principles of Freedom Committee, a group not to be
accused of having suspended judgment. Their attachment
to free institutions, and mine, made the book a joy to write.
I am grateful to the Committee for the help and
encouragement it gave me and for the scrupulous way
in which, after agreeing to support the project,
it left me completely free to write what I would.

Acknowledgment is also gratefully made:
To Paul L. Farris, Ruth Sheldon Knowles, Max Myers,
J. W. Wiley, Leon Wilson, and John Van Sickle, each of whom
gave the entire manuscript a critical reading;

To my graduate students, particularly Dick Edwards,
David Ellsworth, Evan Drummond, and Allan Jacobson,
who read early drafts and helped focus the argument;

To my wife, Eva, and to my two boys, Don and Rob,
for giving over so large a share
of the dinner conversation to economic mythology;

To Purdue University, for lightening my load
so that this book might be written;

To my secretary, Ann Gretencord, for
her skillful editing and typing.

None of the above is held responsible for the views
here expressed; these must be and are my own.

Contents

PART ONE

Myth

CHAPTER ONE

Myth and doctrine

Myth and Doctrine,
Fact and Fable,
Let us sort them
If we're able.

Economics is concerned with the activities of man in supplying his wants. Jobs, prices, production, distribution, consumption, buying, and selling are, therefore, the subject matter of the discipline.

Economics is a mystery to many. Stand on a busy street corner some weekday morning and watch the people streaming by, each occupied with his own affairs. Where are they bound? What are they about? How did they get their present jobs? Who had the forethought to produce the goods with which their needs are probably going to be met?

Or go into a modern supermarket. Here are some 8,000 food items on display, each marked with a price. What forces led to the production of all these items? Why is hamburger 60 cents per pound? Why not 25 or 80? The census lists 1,825 different occupations in the United States, including 264,157 stenographers, 329,903 plumbers, and 37,647 airline pilots. How did we happen to get approximately the right number of people to fill these jobs? A person decides that he needs gas for his car. Who planned that there would be a service station conveniently at hand? Many of these people are displeased with the way things are going; others feel fairly well satisfied. Who or what is responsible for this disappointment, or this satisfaction, or this apathy? Ask these questions of the people themselves and you would get a great variety of answers, partly based on things wholly personal and partly based on economic mythology. That there might be undergirding principles — economic laws — which explain and coordinate this multiplicity of activities would be a novel thought to many. The whole process, marvelously integrated and interdependent as it is, seems without a unifying principle.

There are three major ways of organizing economic activity. One, the oldest, is the "traditional economy," as in much of India today. Another, the "command society," is typified by the slave economies of former days. The most recent, the "exchange economy," is the system of specialization, accompanied by buying and selling, that we find in the United States. The first two are "status" systems, based on authority; the third is a "contract" system, based on freedom. If one were to ask "Why do the people behave as they do?" he would get a different reply in each of these economies. In the traditional society the answer would be simple and easily understood: "Because that is what people have always done." In the command society the answer would also be clear: "Because that is what people are required to do." But in the exchange economy the answer is not so understandable: "They do what they themselves have chosen." This leaves much unexplained. How would 200 million people, operating without central direction, make the proper choices? One can understand the behavior of an unchanging society or the behavior that results from central command. But how explain the functioning of a voluntary system, with each person freely choosing his own job and making

4

his own decisions? The principles that support it are not widely understood. To many people, economics in a society like ours is beyond comprehension.

People do not like to be without comprehension. They like to understand things, to have an explanation, to have some belief that permits an observed event to take on meaning. This craving finds outlet in the myths people create to explain their condition or their hopes or the events they observe about them. The belief does not necessarily have to be true; some fragment of truth will suffice. There is not ordinarily a disposition to place the myth to the test. To do so would be to risk the security of mind the myth provides, which is the purpose of its being. The motive leading to the propagation of a myth is not the scientific quest for fact; it is a subconscious desire for an individually acceptable answer to the question "Why?" With so avid a desire for explanations, with the explanations so plentifully offered and with such poor tests for them, it follows that old myths will have long lives and new myths will constantly be created. The test for an explanation often is its effectiveness in advancing some special cause rather than its veracity as determined by objective appraisal. Thus the fertile breeding ground for new myths.

Economics is especially plagued with myths because this is a field in which everyone considers himself to be an expert. An architect designing an apartment building would not be challenged by the ordinary citizen as to the adequacy of the foundation he plans. The average citizen is not likely to dispute the doctor's diagnosis or the pilot's decision. But the economist enjoys no such shield from public appraisal; he will be challenged on almost every point by people who think their economic sense is better than his.

With everyone qualified, at least in his own mind, to interpret economic events, there arise fragmentary and inconsistent explanations for observed events. And since the events of greatest interest are those that are unusual, many of the economic myths unknowingly deal with the aberration rather than with the norm.

Many of these myths have a literary quality to them. Some have a strong moral tone, and a number have aesthetic attractiveness. All are likely to be provincial, not consistent with one another. Most of them cannot be generalized. The only condition under which any one of them could be true would be a condition of chaos in the larger body of economic principle. Coming as many of them do from the contemplation of a particular situation, they reflect deep-felt attitudes toward vocational callings and toward rival groups. Pride in one's work and identification of one's own goals with the good of society all find their way into the myths. A sense of martyrdom creeps into many of them, reflecting the esteem with which the martyr's role is endowed.

Here are a few typical economic myths, briefly treated:

LABOR MYTHS

"Labor is not a commodity," says the union leader, to loud applause. True, of course. Labor is a service, not a commodity. Courts and legislative bodies have affirmed the distinction between wages and prices, between labor and lumber. But if, by this statement, one means that labor is immune to the economic laws that affect commodities, that is another thing indeed, and a serious error.

The law of supply, which affects commodities, also affects labor. Other things equal, a higher price will result in the production of a larger supply of commodities and a higher wage will attract additional numbers of workers into the labor force. The law of demand, which affects commodities, affects labor in the same way. Other things equal, a higher price will reduce the sales of beef and a higher wage will reduce the sale of labor. If wood increases in price relative to metal, the maker of office furniture is likely to shift to metal. If the cost of labor increases relative to the cost of capital, the manufacturer is likely to put in labor-saving machinery.

The beliefs persist that labor is not affected by conventional economic laws, that the legal minimum wage could be raised without reducing employment, and that the whole wage structure could be lifted without causing the employer to substitute capital for labor. These are myths, believable only in a world characterized by chaos rather than by economic law.

Another labor myth is the belief that large wage increases can be granted out of company profits without increasing the price of the product. This is one myth that can be tested. There are many definitions of profits. Perhaps the one most generally used is the return to capital. With profits thus defined, 1965 was the most profitable year in American history, up to then. Corporate profits after taxes (the returns to capital) in 1965 were $44.5 billion; wages totaled $357.4 billion. If all the returns to capital had been paid out to labor, wages could have gone up some 12 percent. This would have been a catastrophe, not a gain. To erase returns to capital by converting them all to wages would be fatal to industry, wiping out all job opportunities. We would have killed the goose that laid the golden egg.

A myth prominent in the ranks of labor is that the substitution of capital for human muscle reduces the number of jobs and is, therefore, contrary to labor's interest. "Hello steam shovel, goodbye John" was an early expression of this idea. Technocracy, cybernation, and automation are words that characterize the process.

In a given immediate situation, automation cuts down the number of jobs. The adoption of typesetting machines clearly reduced the number of handsetting jobs. But in a broader sense and over a period of time, automation is a creator of jobs, not a destroyer. Typesetting machines made printing so cheap that the use of printed material was vastly expanded, creating many more jobs in the printing business than before.

It is to the interest of the laboring man to have in hand the best tools he can get. With good tools he can be much more efficient; if he is more efficient his employer will bid more for his services.

Another labor myth is the belief that the way to increase employment is to increase wages. The reasoning is clear enough. The cause of unemployment is said to be lack of consumer buying power. If wages are increased, the argument goes, buying power will be greater, more consumer goods will be needed, factories will increase production to supply the market, and additional workers will be needed to supply the added output. Fire burns stick, stick beats dog, dog bites pig, pig jumps over the stile, and all get safely home. Seemingly no flaw in the logic.

That there could be a situation in which this chain of reasoning has validity is not to be doubted. If the employers were making very large profits and stowing these away in the bedticking, the analysis would follow. But if the employers were closer to the break-even point, an increase in wages could put many of them into bankruptcy long before the projected chain of events came to pass.

8

FARM MYTHS

When farmers take their produce to market they generally can only accept or reject the price that is offered. When they go into the store to buy they usually have to pay the price that is asked or go without. The farmer does not get to name a price; the other fellow tells him what the price is. The market economy is felt by many farmers to be singularly perverse as it affects them. The myth has developed that the economic system works to the farmer's disadvantage and indeed has singled him out for mistreatment.

The truth is that the market system has no chosen friends or enemies. It is impersonal in its effect. True, it is easier for the steel industry to control its output and thus influence price than it is for farmers to control their output. And it has been easier for labor to organize and engage in collective bargaining than it has been for farmers. But on the other hand, farmers have more independence than labor, and there is more assurance of a market for beef than there is for Edsel cars or hula hoops.

Farm families received in 1962 only about 60 percent as much income, on the average, as nonfarm families. At the same time, they had four times as much net worth. When one takes account of all the facts, there is hardly a basis for believing that farmers have been singled out for persecution. Yet the myth persists, supporting the greater myth that the economic system is either chaotic or malevolent.

Another agricultural myth holds that price has no effect on consumption — that prices of farm products could be increased or decreased sharply without changing the amount that people would buy.

The flat statement is a dangerous exaggeration. It is true that for most farm products, in the short run, a given price change is associated with a relatively small change in consumption. However, this cannot be generalized for the long run. In the short run a reduced supply of cotton results in a much higher price. But in the long run, if the price of American cotton is held high, the textile trade looks to foreign cotton and to rayon. In the short run a reduced supply of corn leads to a higher price, but in the long run, if corn is held high in price, the livestock industry turns to other feeds and to forage crops. In the short run a reduced supply of turkeys leads to a considerably higher price, but in the long run, if turkeys are kept scarce and high in price, the consumer will turn to ham or broilers.

A person may persist, year after year, in a practice with known favorable short-run consequences. But in time the short run fades into the long run and the short-run analysis is no longer valid. Thus by using short-run analyses as a basis for continuing programs, markets are lost and incomes reduced. Adoption of the price support program for American cotton is the classic example of this kind of error; by taking this approach cotton gave up its markets. While we held American cotton production stable, cotton production in the rest of the world trebled and the production of synthetic fibers skyrocketed. Such is the result of writing economic programs based on myth.

The known short-run effect of a highball is a degree of exhilaration. The long-run effect of repeated highballs is quite different.

The myth that price has no effect on consumption is a

cliché of chaos. If it were true, we would be without any explanation for economic behavior generally. Reliance on this myth is like trying to explain the behavior of the solar system without recourse to the law of gravity.

What a contradictory confusion of claims and counterclaims! In agriculture some hold that a high price reduces consumption; others argue that it does not. Among labor groups some believe that a high wage will reduce the number of jobs; others contend that employment will increase. Economic theory and careful study reveal, however, that the law of demand has general validity: a high price discourages consumption of farm products and a high wage restricts the number of employees a manufacturer will wish to employ. To argue otherwise is to postulate a system that is chaotic and contradictory, subject to no general principle.

BUSINESS MYTHS

The business community is abundantly supplied with myths, and these are quite as provincial in their way as those of agriculture and labor. Thurmond Arnold has written a book of 400 pages on the subject.

One large family of business myth relates to the conditions that explain income and employment. At its baldest, the view is that the generally lower per capita incomes of laboring people are an indication of basic inferiority on the part of these people, and that unemployment is in itself sufficient evidence of a man's unwillingness to work. This myth attributes superior ability and enterprise to members of the business community. In this respect, it is self-serving. As with the other myths, a selected individual instance may appear to give validity to

11

the proposition. But there is no basis for the universality attributed to the myth by many who hold it. Low incomes and unemployment are more a result of poor education and economic slack than of genetic inferiority or laziness.

Another myth of the business community is that a considerable degree of unemployment is desirable because this makes men more worried about their jobs and hence more diligent workmen. This myth rationalizes, allegedly in the public interest, the businessman's desire for an abundant supply of labor at a low wage. However, it expresses poorly the employer's long-run interest; we know from empirical studies that the business community does better when labor is fully employed (and markets are strong) than when people are begging for jobs (and buying power is low).

Similarly, it is believed that if wages are high, the laborer can supply his needs with fewer days of work and will lie down on the job. The myth holds that it is socially disadvantageous to pay wages above some indicated level because if one pays these higher wages the total product diminishes. The idea finds expression in a concept called the "backward-bending supply curve." Empirical evidence in support of this idea is fragmentary and conflicting. Undoubtedly it has validity with respect to the short-run behavior of certain individual persons, but there is little evidence to support it in a generalized form. A particular individual may be inclined to work fewer hours if his hourly wage is increased, but the higher wage will attract additional workers and increase total output. There are good arguments for having wages at a moderate rather than at a very high level, but the alleged adverse impact of high wages on total output is not one of them. The myth lacks sound support on empirical or theoretical grounds. The backward-bending supply curve has its counterpart in agriculture in the myth that with high prices farmers will not be under such heavy pressure to produce and output will decline. No valid research supports this myth.

Another piece of business folklore is the protectionist myth, which holds that trade can be a one-way street, with the country selling abroad but buying only home-produced goods. Such a policy is demonstrably impossible over any length of time. Unless we pay dollars to foreigners for goods they send us, they will never have the dollars with which to buy our exports. Furthermore, a consequence of protectionism is to impose a penalty in the form of a reduced level of living, as the French economist Frederik Bastiat showed in a brilliant piece of logic, written about the middle of the nineteenth century. With tongue in cheek Bastiat offered a petition arguing that sunlight, coming free from outer space, was a low-cost and therefore unfair source of illumination. France would be better off, said he, if all houses were built without windows. Just think of the great benefits that would accrue to his "petitioners," he said, enumerating them as "the manufacturers of Candles, Waxlights, Lamps, Candlesticks, Street Lamps, Snuffers, Extinguishers, and the producers of Oil, Tallow, Rosin, Alcohol, and, generally, of everything connected with Lighting."

The trouble with the protectionist myth is that once one starts down this road there is no logical stopping place. "Buy American" logically gives way to "buy local." Ultimately it becomes an argument against trade in any form. The concept is like the other myths in that it is provincial, incapable of being integrated into a larger explanation.

Many people of the business community who believe strongly in the market have a myth to the effect that the market can solve practically any economic problem. The market is believed to have universal applicability and the businessman un-limited power. "Just put a businessman in charge," the saying goes, "and the problem will be solved." The financial matters of the federal government, educational problems of the state, and the social needs of the local community are presumed to be equally amenable to the market approach.

Indeed, there was a time when the market was used as the solution for most of these problems. Privately owned turnpikes were once built, and the traveler paid a toll every few miles. Wars were fought with mercenaries; during the War Between the States a drafted citizen could hire a man to fight in his stead. In the early days of our country we undertook almost no public intervention in the field of money and credit, leaving everything to an undisciplined market. Even immigration was once a matter for the market, using the institution of inden-tured labor. Education, too, was at one time a matter primarily for the market, available only to those who could pay for it.

But, as judged by a great many people over a long period of time, these private operations did not work satisfactorily. Public programs now reinforce, supplement, or parallel pri-vate business enterprise in all of these areas. The doctrinaire argument for a universal private-market operation has dimin-ished; it is a myth now held only by an articulate few.

Permeating these myths of labor, agriculture, and business, we may note again, are short-run and long-run concepts. In the short run, automation destroys jobs, increased farm output re-duces income, and free trade wipes out business firms. In the long run, automation lifts the level of living, increased farm production creates benefits that are widely distributed, and lib-eral trade policies result in better allocation of resources.

One myth has it that we live forever in the present, that

14

the increments of time are small, and that the long run never really happens. Thus long-range considerations are to be dismissed. "In the long run we are all dead," said John Maynard Keynes, cogently expressing this view. Politicians, whose time horizon is the next election, often have the short-run view, as do many citizens. The future, remote and uncertain, is discounted heavily.

The rival myth is that short-run considerations are of little significance, being merely transitory. If we really understood economic principle, the myth has it, we would see that even during the short run we are working toward the long-run equilibrium in which all things will be optimized. In this view there are few real economic problems other than those the government has created, as, operating from short-run considerations, it impedes the natural equilibrating forces. Many economists are inclined to take this long-run view.

Those who embrace the myth that the long run never happens need to examine a few case histories such as the Stevenson Plan, an effort to reduce the supply and raise the price of rubber in Malaya during the 1920's. This short-run effort indeed raised the price of rubber for the Malayans but in so doing had the long-run effect of losing a good share of the market to their rivals in the Netherlands East Indies. More recently, one might look at the increasing volume of imports that results from high wages and high prices in the steel industry. Continued use of short-run programs phases inevitably into the long run and moves one farther and farther out of adjustment. The pain of adjustment leads to postponing the evil day when reality must be faced — making the evil day that much more evil.

Those, on the other hand, who would ignore the short run should reflect on the fact that if one's short-run difficulties are excessive he will never be around to share the highly praised long-run joys. It is well to point out that overseas investment will, in the long run, ease the balance-of-payments problem, as repatriated earnings increase the inflow of dollars. But the long-run soundness of this analysis loses its relevance if the short-run consequence is total depletion of our reserves. It is well enough to tell the laborer that automation is a long-run blessing, but if it costs him his job he will have little enthusiasm for it. Nor will the textile manufacturer, forced into bankruptcy by imports from Japan, be persuaded to favor liberal trade because it will be good for posterity. The farmer, worried by surpluses and low prices, is not persuaded that abundant supplies have long-run advantages.

What is called for is awareness that *both* short-run and long-run considerations are important. Neither should be embraced as the sole criterion for action — or inaction. We should avoid the preoccupation with the short run that characterized French royalty before the Revolution and led to the saying, "After us the deluge." We should also avoid the disregard of the short run which, during the forced collectivization of agriculture in the Soviet Union, led the state to sacrifice millions of lives in pursuit of long-run goals. The short-run efforts to alleviate distress should be of such a nature as to move *gradually* in the direction indicated by the long-run analysis.

In balancing the short run with the long run we in the United States have succeeded rather well. We have had the genius, as a people, to live in the short-run world and yet to save part of our energies for working in the direction of necessary long-run adjustments. Our many public efforts to solve immediate problems and our steadily rising level of living indicate that in most cases we have steered effectively between the short-run and the long-run myths. For the greater part, we have found a workable blend of the immediate and of the future in which the present provides a better level of living than the past and the future promises another advance.

The myths we have considered to this point have generally been harmful, an obstruction to wise public policy. But there is a family of beneficial myths. Belief validates these myths and makes them useful; disbelief would destroy both the myths and their benefits.

Credit is such a myth. The basis of credit is confidence — confidence that the economy will keep operating successfully, that borrowers will continue to earn income, that they will be able to pay their debts. So long as the belief persists, the myth is validated and the system works well. If doubts arise, if confidence dwindles, the credit structure could collapse like a house of cards, as it did during the Great Depression. Much thought has gone into building safeguards against such doubts. Substantial safeguards have been built. Federal Deposit Insurance for banks is an illustration; it virtually prevents the kind of run on the banking system that would wreck our financial structure. Credit, then, is a myth that is immensely useful so long as it is believed in. It destroys itself — and the economy — when disbelief creeps in.

If one undertakes to purge all economic myths, he runs a great risk indeed. He may destroy what is useful along with what is harmful. Cynicism, pessimism, and disbelief, exercised by a narrowly analytical mind, can so shrink the basis of common agreement as to make any economic system unworkable.

We have been considering the clash between economic myth and economic doctrine, drawing illustrations from a number of areas. However, the honors do not always lie with the theory or the doctrine or the professional economists. Sometimes the folklore and the mythology prove to be superior. The doctrine is then revised, accepting the myth at least in part, and making it respectable. The contest between the "conventional wisdom" and the "onslaught of circumstance" has been well described by the economist John Kenneth Galbraith. Listed below are a number of once respected theories, formerly a part of the accepted economic discipline, even though in disagreement with much popular thought. In time, these theories were rejected; popular thought triumphed and is now reputable doctrine.

The Labor Theory of Value

This theory held that everything was the product of labor. According to it, a thing had value because labor was expended in its production. The whole product of society, therefore, rightly belonged to labor, the theory held, and any share of product going to the owners of land or capital constituted exploitation. The idea appeared two hundred years ago with the classical economists. It was borrowed and developed by Karl Marx, who turned it into a weapon of hate against the propertied class. While it is retained in Communist doctrine, its errors have long been evident (see Chapters Two and Three). The idea, which is contrary to the good sense of many people, has been purged from Western thought. We learned that pearls are not valuable because men dive for them, but men dive for them because they are valuable.

The Iron Law of Wages

This idea held that wages cannot get above the subsistence level; laboring people, it was said, would be held down to grinding poverty by the pressure of population on the food supply. The English economists Malthus and Ricardo subscribed to this belief. The theory helped rationalize the very low wages paid to factory workers in the early days of the industrial revolution. Public revulsion called for reexamination and ultimately led to the overthrow of this idea in industrialized societies. (There are parts of the world, as in the Far East, where this harsh principle still has considerable validity.)

The Wages Fund

This theory, also once professionally respectable, held that at any given time there was a fixed amount of goods and services available for the working class and that this amount would be in some fashion divided among the current number of workmen. Laboring people never accepted the idea and continued to strive for a larger total share of the economy's output, despite the protests of economists that success in their quest was impossible. The idea lost professional repute about one hundred years ago.

Say's Law

J. B. Say, a French economist of the early nineteenth century, outlined what has been called the "theory of markets," more widely known as Say's Law. The law held that the money spent in producing a good would constitute the money with which the good could be purchased. "Thus," said Say, "supply creates its own demand." According to his law, there could be no general overproduction, no general unemployment. The law became part of the accepted body of classical economic doctrine. Unconvinced laymen and economic heretics sniped at it for generations. Finally, during the 1930's, in the midst of the Great Depression, John Maynard Keynes made a dramatic and successful frontal assault on the law and developed an explanation for continuing unemployment. This could come, said he, from excessive savings and an insufficiency of buying power. The Keynesian theory has now generally replaced Say's Law. To many economists this was a great professional advance, the purging of an old error. To some it was a backward step, a capitulation of doctrine to folklore, accommodating the unwillingness of labor to adjust wages downward.

While economic theory has been adjusted to accept at least parts of what was once mythology, the reverse is also true. Some of the less worthy myths have disappeared as a result of the steady pressure of economic thought. Europe was once organized on a feudalistic basis, with a powerful landed aristocracy and a great majority of poverty-stricken serfs. There was a body of mythology in support of this institution. Feudalism was overthrown, however, and the mythology which supported it has all but disappeared. Agrarianism once had the support of a powerful set of myths. But agrarianism, or agricultural fundamentalism as it is sometimes called, is on the retreat, being steadily overcome by economic reasoning.

This is the dynamic record of interaction between mythology and economic theory:

In some sectors economic doctrine was once faulty. Ideas regarded as myth helped to purge the theory of its errors and the formerly scorned folklore won its way into the body of respected economic thought.

In several areas economic doctrine has triumphed over

folklore; the myths have receded and are no more than a historical curiosity.

In other areas useful myth supports successful enterprise.

In yet another, and very large area, economic doctrine helps to hold the lid on a Pandora's box filled with a warring assortment of half-truths, untruths, myths, fallacies, fables, and nonsense. The service done society by this policing action is indescribably great.

No man can foretell when this Pandora's box may allow one of the myths to escape. A number have done so; some of these have been captured and exterminated, some are yet at large in the world, while others have been converted to respectability. The myth that increasing wages lead to greater employment already has much professional acceptance. The backward-bending supply curve seems on the verge of becoming professionally acceptable. Who can say what change in the economy or what change in the public mood might release one of the myths yet held in captivity?

The opinions of professional economists seldom wholly concur; they are continually changing, sometimes greatly but often only gradually. Professors of economics, it is said, need not change their examination questions from one year to the next; it is sufficient that they change the answers.

In this evolving process, some consensus is needful. In the Communist world there is no question as to what is dogma and what is myth. These are as they were given by Marx or Lenin. Any needed interpretation comes from a designated public official. In the Western world there is no such authority. The professional journals probably come as near being decisive on matters of economic theory as is possible in a free society. In the United States this would be the *American Economic Review;* in England it has long been the *Economic Journal.*

The evolution of theory is, of course, a controversial process. To the casual observer it seems that economists are always in disagreement. This is an illusion. Economists see little worth discussing in the 95 percent of their subject matter on which they agree; most of the discussion concerns the 5 percent in which myth and doctrine are in disagreement.

The economist will abhor myths if he is essentially of a conservative frame of mind. If he is a progressive, he will scrutinize them carefully, in search of such folk wisdom as they might have.

This struggle between myth and doctrine is dynamic and useful. Were it not for the continued questioning of both myth and doctrine, the discipline would either become stagnant, tied to an outmoded earlier time, or would explode in a burst of nonsense. Some myths are stumbling blocks to progress; others are the promises that men live by. To identify them correctly is the challenge of the professional economist and the intelligent layman, interacting with one another.

The body of economic thought cannot be reduced to a limited list of empirically demonstrated economic laws. This is too narrow a base from which to operate. For an economy to function successfully, there must be some belief, some myth, some commitment, beyond what is clearly demonstrable. If there were no economic myths, it would be necessary to invent some.

The relationships between economic theory and practice deserve consideration before we close this chapter. This is the usual sequential relationship of the two: People, dealing with some practical problem, act with intuition, folk wisdom, inventiveness, and experimentation. Through such knowledge as they have and through trial and error, they devise some solution, some institution, some mode of action that is distinguished by the fact that *it works*. This may be a credit institution, it may be a currency system, or it may be a method of settling international balances. Along comes the economic theorist, a very gifted man and a rare specimen indeed. As with poets and composers, there may not be more than a single really good one in a generation. His qualifications are superb. He is thoroughly schooled in economic theory. He is a keen observer. He is courageous and inventive, endowed with insight. He studies this new thing that people have done and elucidates the economic sense of it. He draws on the existing body of economic theory and extends it, with necessary modifications, into this new area. He articulates the economic principles that have made the venture successful, and he shows why other ventures, differently based, have failed. Most important, his discovery makes possible the elaboration and extension of the new venture; now that the principles are known, the undertaking may be projected much farther and much more fruitfully.

Thus, long before there was any economic theory, people learned to exchange goods. The economic theorist, with his insight, described how and why this system was successful. The principles he articulated, once known, made possible the extension of the market in its many modern complexities.

A modern illustration may be helpful. Recently, practical people, plagued with the concurrent problems of surplus agricultural commodities and unmet needs for food, devised what is variously known as Public Law 480, the Agricultural Trade and Development Act, and "Food For Peace." Essentially this is a venture in large-scale international donation, or, as sometimes stated, "unilateral transfers" or "unrequited sales." There are some side effects relating to commercial export sales, foreign agricultural production, and domestic farm policy. There has been no formal body of economic theory to give guidance on unrequited sales; the theory of economics is based on payment and value received. There were a few general principles that had some applicability. In working out Public Law 480, the drafters called in the best economists available, for counsel. All opposed it; the plan had a flimsy or nonexistent theoretical basis. Nevertheless, the program was launched. The political and administrative inventors, faced with a new and very real problem, built an institution that seems to work. Now come the economic theorists, building, bit by bit, the theoretical fabric which shows how and why it works. Equipped with this knowledge, the practitioners are now able to improve their instrument and to predict more accurately the conditions under which it will and will not function.

There is popular feeling that "theory" is opposed to "practice" and that the merits lie with "practice." This is a false conclusion, based on a false supposition. If practice has long been successful and does not conform to theory, the theory is bad and in need of revision. If practice is costly, inefficient, and not in conformity with theory, the practice is wrong and in need of change. The fact that there is so much popular criticism of theory is simply evidence that much of what is considered good theory is really nothing more than bad myth.

There is nothing more practical than good theory and there is nothing more sound theoretically than good practice. The distinction should not be between theory and practice; it should be between good theory and bad theory, between good practice and bad practice. If both theory and practice are good, they will conform to one another, particularly in the long run.

24

Practice is brick; theory is mortar. Both are essential and both must be good if we are to erect a worthy structure.

John Maynard Keynes, who will be quoted a number of times in this book, commented thus in his *General Theory* (page 383):

> . . . ideas of economists and political philosophers, both when they are right and when they are wrong, are more powerful than is commonly understood. Indeed the world is ruled by little else. Practical men, who believe themselves to be quite exempt from any intellectual influences, are usually the slaves of some defunct economist. Madmen in authority, who hear voices in the air, are distilling their frenzy from some academic scribbler of a few years back. I am sure that the power of vested interests is vastly exaggerated compared with the gradual encroachment of ideas.

CHAPTER TWO

The myth that if someone gains, someone else loses

If a hungry man has water,
And a thirsty man has bread,
Then, if they trade, be not dismayed,
They both come out ahead.

The belief that probably causes the most difficulty in the field of public policy is this: if two people engage in a transaction and one of them is seen to gain thereby, it must follow that the other has lost. This myth is extended to encompass whole groups. If the business community, in dealing with farmers, is seen to prosper, the myth indicates that the farmers must have lost. It is extended even further, to cover international trade. If Belgium has trade with Africa and visibly improves her position thereby, the myth holds that this improvement must have come at the expense of Africa. Economics is looked on as a game of dice; no greater value is carried away than is brought in. Let us investigate this proposition.

Consider two common characterizations of the exchange process. In the first one, the average citizen drives past the suburban home of some wealthy businessman, notes the huge lawn, the lovely landscaping, and the late-model car parked in the driveway. "Nobody," says he to himself, "could get that much money without taking it away from somebody else."

In the second characterization, this same citizen buys a

pair of shoes at a drygoods store owned by the same business-man. "Thank you," he says, as he receives his shoes. "Thank you," says the clerk as he rings up the money. Is this exchange of "thank you's" a mere matter of form? Or does it express something intuitively or even subconsciously felt by these two people? In any case, buyer and seller have cause to be pleased with this voluntary transaction. Each received an item of greater value *to him* than the value of the item with which he parted. The buyer preferred the shoes to the money; for the seller the reverse was true. Both gained by the exchange.

Which of these two characterizations is the more accurate, the citizen's allegation that he has been exploited, or his courteous acknowledgment of a service rendered? Is the exchange process mutually advantageous? Or is it a matter of exploitation? The myth says that trade is exploitation — exploitation of the weaker by the stronger, of the smaller by the larger, of the poorer by the more wealthy. There is an understandable basis for the view that someone's gain is someone else's loss. If Notre Dame plays Purdue and wins, Purdue obviously loses. If one man wins the election, his rival clearly loses. By this same reasoning, if two men do business with one another and the one is seen to prosper, the other must have lost.

Trade may indeed involve exploitation, as we shall see. But this is not necessarily so, or even frequently so. The most common occurrence is that both parties gain.

This is easy to see in barter, which is the prototype for all voluntary exchange. Tom Sawyer trades a fishhook to his friend Billy in exchange for a yellow Sunday School ticket. Tom prefers the ticket to the fishhook and Billy prefers the exact opposite. So they trade, voluntarily, and each is better off.

The principle is the same when it involves money, except that it then becomes more obscure. An assembly-line worker in Indiana earns his pay by making a part for an automobile built in Detroit and sold in New Jersey. He spends his money for a watch put together in Chicago from parts made in Switzerland. What is his relationship to each of the other people involved? It is difficult to describe accurately, even with all the tools available to the economic analyst. How much simpler it is to conclude that whoever seems to prosper in this process must have done so at the expense of the others!

George Foster, a social scientist, says that individuals in the less-developed countries are often disinclined to adopt changes because of group pressures arising from the belief that one man's gain is another man's loss. The peasant regards another man's success as achieved at his expense, Foster says, and he discourages his neighbor from innovating.

Most of us studied at some time or another the idea that matter and energy can neither be created nor destroyed. The thought carries over to the realm of economics and appears in the form of the myth now under study. Utility, or usefulness, the myth implies, is a constant amount, some ceiling quantity that cannot be added to but can only be transferred from hand to hand. If someone has more of it, according to the myth, someone else must have less. The valid law of the conservation of energy is carried over, incorrectly, into a false law of the conservation of utility. Repeated endlessly, the myth creeps into the thinking of people who should know better. A government official says that we should engage in trade with the Communists only when the advantage is on our side. He is in the grip of the myth; if there is trade, both sides are likely to gain. A man hears that his friend traded cars. "Who got the best of the deal?" he asks, which is the wrong question. If it was a voluntary transaction, both parties probably did well. It is impossible to give the right answer to the wrong question; the tragedy is that we spend so much of our time asking the wrong question and trying to answer it!

Theoretical economics has a phrase which expresses the thought that if someone gains, someone else loses: "the zero sum game." This phrase aptly expresses the idea that shifting goods or services from one pair of hands to another will leave their total usefulness unchanged. This is a convenient idea and enhances the maneuverability of economic data, but it is at odds with the facts.

Once the myth is embraced, many things follow. All profits become evil, all business is viewed as a scramble to take something away from somebody else, and all wealth is thought to have been accumulated by exploitation. Any nation that really accepts this myth will either confiscate or closely regulate its private property, will inject government deeply into the marketing and pricing process, and will substitute centralized decision-making for the operation of free markets. The fact that the United States has gone far in this direction is evidence that the myth is widely held. The danger to a free society bred by this myth is subtle and great.

In order to understand the errors in the myth, it is necessary to examine the exchange process as the economist does.

In an exchange economy such as we have in the United States, people produce a limited number of goods and services which they sell, receiving money in payment. This money they use to buy the many goods and services they desire and can afford. A typical person in the American economy will produce and sell one or two goods or services; the money he receives will be used to buy untold thousands of other items.

This system of specialization and exchange has immense natural efficiencies. It calls for investment in factories and machine tools, permitting mass production, large-scale merchandising, and other highly efficient practices. The average American in our exchange economy has a per capita income 80 times as high as the average citizen of Malawi, with its traditional society, in which each family produces directly for its own needs. The process of specialization and trade is more the engine of human betterment than it is a means of exploitation.

It is clear that as specialization and trade take place, the total volume of wealth increases. Concurrently, with widespread trading, the net worth of the country is rising. Thus the gross evidence is contrary to the myth.

Experience shows that when people are free to exchange goods, they invariably do so. If, as the myth would have it, one party or the other is victimized in this process, it would be most extraordinary that the total population would so consistently lay itself open to injury.

Events of the day cut the ground out from under the proposition, as any discerning person will readily see. For example, the myth holds that the European powers enriched themselves and impoverished their colonies through trade. If this were indeed true, the colonial people should have been poorer than those not colonized. Such was not the case. Furthermore, when independence was achieved and the trade ties were broken, the new countries should have surged forward and the European countries should have experienced recession. Neither of these things happened.

Much of the myth about exploitation in the exchange process comes through certain beliefs regarding price. The feeling is that if a "fair" price could somehow be established, the alleged exploitation would cease and trade could be carried on without unmerited gain or undeserved loss.

The search for a "fair price" or a "just price" was a major concern of the Church during the economy of the Middle Ages. The modern quest for a fair price is a secular one but is subject to the same errors as were encountered hundreds of years ago.

Some people collect salt shakers. Others collect stamps or old guns. I collect definitions of a fair price. Here are a number of examples, all having some merit but also some defect:

(1) "A fair price is one that will permit a stated return on the investment." This criterion is used by regulatory bodies in establishing railroad freight rates and public utility charges. It works reasonably well for a static industry. But a 5 or 6 percent return is too small for the electronics industry which, in the public interest, needs to expand rapidly. On the other hand, it is too much for the buggy industry, which needs to contract.

(2) "A fair price is 10 percent more." This standard was offered some years ago by B. H. Hibbard of the University of Wisconsin. With cynicism and realism, it characterizes the understandable but insatiable appetite of producer groups for a higher price.

(3) "A fair price is 10 percent less." This criterion, opposite to the one above, is used subconsciously by consumer groups. While we may regard this unreasoned view with lifted eyebrow, it describes accurately the motivation that leads to lower costs and greater efficiency.

(4) "A fair price is a price which permits the seller an adequate level of living." This standard has the support of many good-willed people. The difficulty is that when price is determined with respect to the level of reward rather than with regard to the need for product, we may wind up doing without — or having the product run out of our ears.

(5) "A fair price is a price which permits the buyer to have an adequate level of living." The motivation leading to ad-

vocacy of this criterion is above reproach, but good motive is not enough. For example, this standard was used to hold down the price of wheat in India during a short crop. It resulted in the too-rapid use of existing stocks and failure to attract needed supplies from distant regions. Hunger and starvation resulted; a "fair" price is scant comfort when there is nothing to buy.

(6) "A fair price is a price which permits the manufacturer to pay an adequate wage." Again, the motivation behind this idea is usually good, but the idea often works out poorly. With this criterion we force the manufacturer to pay the same wages in the South as in the North, thereby retarding industrialization of the South. Likewise, on this basis we exclude Japanese imports because, we say, the Japanese manufacturer does not pay his workers adequately. Whether he will be in position to pay them better when one of his markets is cut off is not ordinarily brought into the discussion.

(7) "A fair price is a price which results from the active competition of many sellers." This is a means of guarding against the monopolist, the single seller, but it is not always applicable. We may say, on this basis, that the prices charged by ALCOA, Standard Oil, or U. S. Steel are not fair prices because each of these firms has some degree of monopoly power. As we shall see, the real question is not whether the sellers in a certain industry are few in number, but whether other firms are free to enter the market, to produce and sell.

(8) "A fair price is a price which results from the active competition of many buyers." This is a means of combatting the monopolist, the single buyer. It is a useful concept, but it, too, has its shortcomings. We may say, on this basis, that the price paid by the A & P food chain for meat is not a fair price because there are so few chain store buyers of meat. But again, the real question is not whether the actual buy-

ers are few in number but whether other potential buyers are free to enter the market.

(9) "A fair price is a retail price fixed by a manufacturer." This criterion comes from an effort by businessmen to eliminate cutrate sales and discount houses. "Retail Price Maintenance," it is called, or "Fair Pricing." There has been an effort to give this criterion the respectability of statutory law. To do so would be to condone the cartel and to choke off competition. Attaching the word "fair" to this kind of law would be to travesty an honored word.

(10) "A fair price is the same price that everybody else charges." If conformity is a virtue, this criterion is pure gold. This view of pricing comes from the "establishment," and is directed equally at what is called "chiseling" and "gouging." It involves "gentlemen's agreements" among people who are not necessarily gentlemen.

(11) "A fair price is whatever price has long prevailed." This idea emphasizes stability and shows respect for things long established. In fact, it means rigor mortis in the economic sector.

(12) "A fair price is a price fixed by a group of honest public officials." To people who believe that good intentions are sufficient for any purpose and that majority vote is the ultimate criterion in all matters, this is an acceptable standard. But most of us have seen enough of central decision-making to recognize it as fallible.

(13) "A fair price is a price which has stayed in line with other prices." An example is the parity standard, used in the pricing of farm products. It comes from the idea that a price ratio is likely to be more meaningful than a fixed price. But this criterion, too, is badly flawed. According to this view, if a bushel of wheat bought a pair of overalls when Grandfather was young, a bushel of wheat should be so priced as

to buy a pair of overalls today. This neglects changes in the demand for wheat and overalls and in the costs of producing both.

(14) "A fair price is a price equal to the cost of production plus a reasonable profit." Behind this idea is the valid economic principle that in the long run in a generally stable economic situation, the price of a commodity tends to equal its cost of production, including a return for venturesomeness. But in the short run and in a dynamic situation, this criterion can yield meaningless answers. How figure production cost in the first place? Whose cost of production — the efficient, the average, or the inefficient? And does it matter that the public may need an increase in production, or a decrease? The real determinant of the value of an article in the exchange process is its utility, its capacity to yield satisfaction. In the short run this may or may not be closely related to the cost of its production. It may have cost three dollars to get a Christmas tree to the sales lot, but the value of an unsold tree on December 26 is certainly not related to its cost.

(15) "A fair price is a price which stays within guidelines based on the increase in labor productivity." This is the criterion for a fair price contained in the *1966 Economic Report of the President*. The criterion is a narrow one; omitted from consideration are such major factors as the general tide of inflation or deflation and the unique interaction of supply and demand as they affect a particular firm. It is a criterion better suited to the accountant and the administrator than to the businessman or the economist. Adherence to this criterion over a period of years would mean failure properly to allocate productive resources, resulting in shortages and surpluses.

(16) "A fair price is a price which accurately reflects the amount of socially useful labor that has gone into producing the good or service in question." This is the Marxist concept of pricing. By this principle, wheat produced on poor land

should be priced higher than wheat of equal quality grown on good land, because it required more labor. Land, in this concept, is not considered as deserving any reward. The approach makes pricing a matter of accounting and record-keeping. Since it does not equate supply and demand, the allocation of resources and the rationing of consumption are functions left to administrative decision.

The significant thing about all of the foregoing criteria is this: they all would deprive people of their freedom in the offering or buying of goods and services. While each of the criteria has some degree of merit, they all restrict access to the market in substantial degree. At the root of all this intervention in the processes of the market is acceptance of the myth that free trade is synonymous with exploitation.

The definition I prefer is this: "A fair price is a price which prevails when buyers and sellers generally have free access to the market." This criterion emphasizes the opportunity for individual persons to maximize their satisfaction through voluntary trade. By this criterion, the standard against which to measure the pricing process is the institutional arrangement rather than the immediate price that results. The emphasis is on freedom. The word *freedom* is here used in the constitutional sense — a concept that so limits the freedom of each as to maximize the freedom of all. A serious error comes from considering freedom to be synonymous with license, the total absence of restraint. A better concept of freedom is that it be closely tied to responsibility. The plain citizen puts it simply enough: "Your freedom ends where my rights begin." The more responsibility is self-imposed, the less restraint will have to be supplied from outside. Certainly it is within the province of government to prescribe the general conditions under which access to the market is to be available — conditions related to health, public safety, national security, patent rights, and the like. But arbitrary exclusion from the market does not fit the criterion.

To argue for free access to the market is to contemplate an active but not a dominant role for government. This role is to improve the functioning of the exchange system, to place a floor over the pit of disaster, to help the individual equip himself better for his task as a decision-maker, and to see that the market functions as an enlightened institution.

Many who believe in access to the market allow themselves to be backed into a corner where they have to defend a system that is not at all what they propose. They unintentionally take on the defense, not of the free market, but of a caricature thereof. They are maneuvered into defending the free market not as it is or as it could be, but as it once was or as its adversaries contend it would be.

What is advocated in my preferred definition is a market free in a modern rather than an archaic sense. This means a market free from manipulation, free from misrepresentation, free from gross ignorance, free from senseless gyration, and free from government domination. It means the kind of market that intelligent people are capable of creating in the modern day.

Advocacy of access to the market need not and should not be a doctrinaire position that renounces all of the enlightened marketing institutions that have developed since the turn of the century, though adversaries of the free market try to force defenders into such a position.

If the advantages of the market are to be retained, the myth that makes the market synonymous with exploitation will have to be dispelled. If the abuses latent in the uninhibited operation of the market are to be avoided, the market must be a more enlightened institution. In any case, economic education must occur. The market system at least deserves to be under-stood before it is condemned.

If fact and logic are so strongly against it, how is it that the myth which identifies the market with exploitation is so persis-tent? It must be that it has some basis.

There are indeed some transactions in which one man's gain is another's loss. Here are typical ones:

> A used-car dealer unloads a painted-up but worn-out car on an unsuspecting buyer.
>
> A plantation owner requires his tenants to buy their supplies at his own store, at prices above the competitive level.
>
> A buyer fails to pay his debt.
>
> An employee, having achieved seniority and hence security, "retires on the job" while still drawing his pay.
>
> Several business firms get together and submit identical bids on a construction job, all of them high.
>
> A speculator in the commodity market contracts to sell a commodity which he does not own, starts a bearish rumor, and then buys his contract back after the price has fallen.
>
> A trade group succeeds in getting legislation passed that restricts competition from abroad.
>
> A labor union forces a featherbedding rule upon the employer.

The list obviously could be lengthened at will. In each of these cases one party or the other falls short of obtaining "value received." These abuses of the market, all committed in the name of "freedom," have high visibility; each will be remem-bered and used to characterize the exchange system even though a thousand subsequent transactions turn out well. It is human nature to observe and generalize from the unusual.

Note that these instances of exploitation come from falsification, from the rigging of institutions, or from excluding someone from the market. The remedy, then, should be to open up the market and to improve its functioning. Too often the proposed remedy is to substitute central command for the market forces.

Students of biology learn that there are three distinct circumstances within which different species exist together. Let us examine them briefly because they have their counterparts in the economic system.

There is the competitive relationship, as when corn and weeds compete with each other for moisture and sunlight. There is the parasitic relationship, as when the mistletoe attaches itself to the oak and lives by exploiting its host. There is the symbiotic relationship, by which two species help one another, as do the bee and the clover, the clover providing honey for the bee and the bee helping the clover to set seed.

Failure to understand these relationships has led man to drive to the point of extinction certain species wrongly felt to be harmful. We are now discovering that some relationships thought to be parasitic or competitive are not so in fact and that the number of symbiotic relationships is greater than once believed.

The myth that the tradesman is a parasite or an obstacle to well-being has placed in jeopardy an institution that holds immense possibilities for improving levels of living. The need is to dispel this myth and make the market an even more effective instrument.

Lurking in the myth regarding gains and losses is the belief that good can come only when good is deliberately intended. Motive is thought to be the necessary and sufficient explanation for any event. By this reasoning, the clover could gain nothing from the bee because the bee was acting through self-interest. By this analysis the tradesman could not be associated with any gain on the part of his customer unless it was his deliberate intent that the customer should gain.

Motive is important, and the human inclination to search it out is a wise one. But the relationship between motive and consequence is not one-to-one. We are coming to see that good intentions are not enough and occasionally observe that Hell is paved with them. A truth harder to grasp is this: that public good of an economic kind often results from individual self-interest. Economic gains are few enough in this world. We should not reject them, even though they may result from selfish motives.

Now, finally, we come to a subject which is at least as much in the field of psychology as in economics. And, as often is the case when we consider the psychological discipline, we may here be close to something vital.

We have been assuming that the question a person asks when he considers entering into a transaction is this: "Will I be better off than I was before?" Economics is capable of giving help in answering this question. But there is another question, more psychological than economic, imbued not only with self-interest but tinted also with jealousy, a question which poses the invidious comparison: "Will I gain relative to the party with whom I trade?" If this is the criterion, then a transaction can be good, from A's viewpoint, if A gains more than B, or if A gains nothing while B loses, or if A loses less than B. The ideal trade, from A's viewpoint, would be one in which he gains while B loses.

40

Judged by this criterion, *no* transaction can be good for both parties. It is possible, indeed likely, that each gains absolutely. However, it is impossible that each gains relative to the other. Quite probably, part of the dissatisfaction with the market system comes from the fact that some people ask not only that the market produce *absolute gains* for them, but *relative gains* as well. If we consider relative gains instead of absolute gains, then it is indeed true that one man's gain is another man's loss. However, this is an indictment, not of the market, but of the one who asks the impossible.

CHAPTER THREE

The myth that to reward people equally is to treat them fairly

Will joy increase and grief diminish
If we rig the race for a photo finish?

The ethical ideal of equal treatment is deeply rooted. In the Judeo-Christian teaching people are equal before God. Under the American Constitution they are entitled to equal treatment before the law. By common courtesy they are entitled, equally, as persons, to the respect of their fellows. As a result of centuries of struggle, discrimination has been strongly assaulted and we now stand closer to acknowledging equality in these key areas than ever before.

But belief in these fundamental equalities carries over into the idea that people have identical needs and desires, and that equality should be extended to economic rewards. The drive for equal rewards seems an obvious extension of the successful and honored trend toward equality of opportunity. It finds its way into the programs of many labor groups, professional societies, and trade organizations.

The progressive income tax represents an effort to reduce the inequality of rewards. Rates for the top bracket are at 70 percent. Exemptions are provided for those at the low end of the scale. Thus those who receive high incomes are prevented from using the whole of what they earn, while those who receive low incomes have their real rewards increased through social services provided for them from taxes laid on the well-to-do. Another effort to reduce the inequality of rewards is to be found in our welfare programs, federal, state, and local, the outlay for which in 1961 totaled $58 billion, about seven times as much as in 1940.

Organized labor strives for wage rates that are the same for men working on the same job, without reference to performance. Piecework, which results in differential rewards, is rapidly retreating. Industry-wide bargaining represents another drive for equal rewards. So does the minimum wage. Geographic wage differentials are resisted, another manifestation of equal rewards as an objective. In agriculture, parity of income is a frequently stated policy goal; the idea is that average incomes of farm people should be equal to the average incomes of nonfarmers. The tobacco program has long moved in the direction of equal rewards; acreage allotments of the large growers have been reduced and this acreage distributed among small growers. One-third of the growers of Burley tobacco have allotments of one acre or less. The Agricultural Conservation Program has an equalizing feature in its payments to operators of small farms.

Despite these efforts, rewards in the United States continue to be very unequal. In 1960 about 5 percent of our families received less than $1,000 of income from all sources, while about 14 percent received $10,000 or more, as Table I shows. During the past fourteen years incomes have generally risen; note that even after allowing for inflation (income figures represent buying power, not actual dollar income) the percentage of families receiving $10,000 or more has approximately doubled, while the percentage receiving $1,000 or less has been sharply reduced.

TABLE I

Percent of Families Receiving Various Amounts of Income in the United States, in Dollars of Constant Value, 1947 to 1960

	Under $1,000	$1,000 to $1,999	$2,000 to $2,999	$3,000 to $3,999	$4,000 to $4,999	$5,000 to $5,999	$6,000 to $6,999	$7,000 to $9,999	$10,000 and over
1947	7.7	11.4	14.8	16.8	15.3	10.8	6.6	10.5	6.1
1948	8.4	11.4	14.9	17.7	15.7	10.5	6.8	9.4	5.2
1949	9.7	11.6	14.6	17.5	15.3	9.8	6.7	9.9	4.9
1950	9.4	10.4	13.2	16.3	15.7	11.0	7.5	10.7	5.7
1951	8.1	9.8	13.0	16.3	16.7	11.1	8.7	11.0	5.4
1952	7.6	9.6	12.1	16.3	15.3	11.9	9.3	12.2	5.8
1953	7.9	8.9	10.3	13.3	15.3	12.5	10.0	14.4	7.3
1954	8.1	10.0	10.6	13.5	14.9	11.8	9.5	14.1	7.5
1955	7.0	9.0	9.9	12.6	14.2	12.4	10.3	16.3	8.3
1956	6.1	8.1	9.4	11.2	13.6	12.7	10.8	18.2	10.0
1957	6.1	8.1	9.3	11.0	13.4	13.7	10.9	17.8	9.6
1958	5.5	8.6	9.7	11.0	13.3	13.4	10.8	17.3	10.3
1959	5.1	8.3	9.3	10.1	11.7	13.2	11.0	19.0	12.3
1960	5.1	8.1	8.9	10.0	10.8	12.9	10.7	19.7	13.8

Source: Herman P. Miller, "Trends in the Income of Families and Persons in the United States, 1947–1960," U. S. Department of Commerce, Bureau of the Census, Technical Paper No. 8, 1963.

Despite an upward movement of income, the general pattern of income distribution has not been appreciably changed during this recent span of years. The top 5 percent of our families, as Table II shows, received about 17 percent of the country's total income throughout this period. In other words, an average family from the top 5 percent received between three and four times as much income as the average of all families, and this relationship has been quite stable for a considerable period of time.

TABLE II

Percent of the Nation's Income Received by Those Families Whose Incomes Were in the Top Five Percent, 1947–1960

Year	Percent	Year	Percent
1947	17.5	1954	16.4
1948	17.1	1955	16.8
1949	16.9	1956	16.4
1950	17.3	1957	15.8
1951	16.9	1958	15.8
1952	17.7	1959	16.3
1953	15.8	1960	16.9

Source: Same as the preceding table.

Note that the fundamental equalities of religion, constitutional law, and of society are all liberating, concerned with opportunity, and that none of them conveys the idea of equal rewards. Equality before the law does not mean that the law-abiding citizen and the wrongdoer share equally in freedom or in the jail sentence. Equal respect means only that everyone begins with a clean slate, his performance to be judged without prejudice. Equality before God, the law, and one's fellows is the equivalent of an equal place at the starting line. On the other hand, equality of rewards is insistence that all runners breast the tape at the same instant. The two concepts are entirely different, not just in degree but in character. Nevertheless, the compulsive drive toward equal rewards surges on, fueled by the myth that equality is equity.

The important thing about rewards is not whether they are equal but whether they are reasonably related to the contribution and circumstances of each person. As a child, I became ill by trying to eat as much pie as my bigger brother. The proper criterion for me was not whether my piece of pie was as

46

big as my brother's, but whether it was suited to my situation.

A group of individuals may all receive the same rewards, but may all have their freedom infringed and be required to surrender things of greater value than the rewards they receive. Their equality consists in that they are equally exploited. The fact that their rewards are equal in no sense indicates that they are being treated fairly. A group of extortionists may divide their plunder into equal portions, which would indeed be a malpractice of equity.

Obviously an economist is not the person to render the final opinion on the question of rewards. Judgment on what is or is not to be considered fair is a matter for the student of ethics, the moral philosopher, and the voting public. But the economist nevertheless has something worthy to contribute to this discussion. He, better than anyone else, has been able to measure the satisfaction that a person experiences from such rewards as are received. He can predict with some accuracy how a society will function with different systems of rewards. He can tell the social planner something about the directional influence and the strength of forces that must be overcome if a given system of rewards is to be instituted.

It is necessary here, in order to examine the myth that equal rewards constitute fair treatment, that we take up one of the deepest problems in economics — the subject of utility.

The utility of a good or service is its ability to satisfy wants. Measurement of satisfaction is an extremely difficult undertaking. As has been said, the economist has come as close as anyone to achieving it. He does this by observing what people do, how they spend their money, and how in their buying habits they prefer one article to another. Significantly, the economist does not make these determinations by noting what people say. The tongue is a notorious deceiver in these matters, counting among its chief victims the very person whose views it undertakes to express.

Why do I like sharp cheese? Probably because I ate it in my youth and came to like its taste. Other people think sharp cheese is for the mouse trap. Why do I want a fountain pen with a broad point? Because it pleases me to write a forceful, vigorous script; it releases something I want to express. I have a friend who chooses a pen with a fine point and writes so faintly that his hand is barely legible.

During World War II the Army rationed cigarettes. For the heavy smokers this was a great hardship. For the non-smokers it was a great folly. Sugar was likewise rationed. Who would claim that a pound of sugar equally satisfies the wants of the baby, the banker, the bartender, and the diabetic? I know two people in the $7,000-income class with markedly different aims. For one of them an extra dollar is so important that he is about to take a second job. The other seems satisfied with his income and makes no apparent effort to increase it.

Suppose that the dollar incomes of all citizens were somehow made equal. What, then, after this equality had been achieved, would be the utility or the satisfaction added by increasing the now equal individual incomes, across the board, by some given amount? For those who had long been accustomed to poverty and had already experienced a sharp increase in income, the satisfaction added by increasing their incomes by yet another increment would be very little; the equalized income was so much above their established level that a further increase would hardly be significant. On the other hand, those who had been wealthy and had had their incomes reduced would wish to reestablish the higher level of living to which they had earlier become accustomed; the satisfaction added by some increment to income would be considerable. Stated in economic language, if incomes were equalized, there would still be enormous variation, from person to person, in the marginal utility of a dollar.

One can argue that cheese is cheese, a pen is a pen, and a dollar is a dollar, and that to confer these objects equally on the populace would be to dispense equal satisfaction. However, this is one of the gravest analytical fallacies of which we are capable. It would be true only if all men were identical, depersonalized robots. The error of this idea is quickly demonstrated in the observed fact that wherever goods and services are rationed out equally, a market springs up for the interchange of these goods. Motivation for such a market comes from the marvelous diversity in the wants and habits of individuals.

Equal rewards, then, give unequal satisfaction. If we ever should bring about a situation in which rewards were equal, we can be certain of one thing: we would be an unhappy people. The wiser heads among the social planners realize this. They reject the idea of equal rewards and strive for a society that rewards people not *equally* but *according to their needs*. To those intent upon such an objective, the basic idea is to bring about *equal degrees* of satisfaction. Suppose someone were to invent a marvelous instrument, a satisfaction meter, that would permit us to take precise mental readings from the population. The objective of idealistic social planners would be that such an instrument should give the same reading for each person, or at least that the reward conferred should advance satisfactions for each person by the same amount. For me a high reading might be given by a combination that included, among other things, greasy fried potatoes, a good lawn, plenty of books, a good supply of wood for my fireplace, and an occasional theater ticket. For someone else it might include a late-model car and an abundant supply of liquor. For yet another it might include lots of open air, plenty of leisure, and a fishpole. For one with a light heart, a given degree of satisfaction might be achieved with a small reward indeed. For a man who was more acquisitive, the reward would have to be very large. For the morose no reward could bring the satisfaction meter's reading up to the standard level. Indeed, only some of life's satisfactions are related to rewards conferred in the form of goods and services. It is still true that the best things in life are free.

How can anyone tell what will give utility or satisfaction to another person? As parents we know our children intimately, yet how well are we able to anticipate their satisfactions? How many parents have seen the child fling aside the shiny new toy that had been so carefully selected, and turn to some battered old treasure? With this example in mind, consider the difficulty of trying to determine the separate utility of many thousands of different items for 200,000,000 people. And, if it were possible to determine these satisfactions, imagine the difficulties of setting up the machinery to make the appropriate distribution!

The sheer impossibility of solving this problem causes the social planner to fall back on the thing that *is* administratively feasible, namely, to pass out equal numbers of dollars, equal packages of cigarettes, and equal amounts of sugar. Convincing people that this is equal treatment is a triumph of propaganda and an affront to individual dignity.

The believer in the free society has his own answer to the problem of rewards. "Who," he asks, "can know the satisfaction conveyed by a good or service better than the individual in question? Why should some central agency try to prescribe

50

rewards? Why try to make them equal? Why not let each individual undertake the quest for such amount of income as he thinks needful, assuring him an equal opportunity, along with others? And why not allow him to spend his income in accordance with his own value standards?"

Indeed, says the believer in the market economy, if rewards were made equal, there would be no incentive for production. Here he has a very strong point. The whole argument about equal rewards, says the economist, takes production for granted. While we were trying to cut the melon and divide it fairly among the company, no one would have the incentive to produce another melon. There is abundant evidence to support this view, beginning in early times and coming on up to the present. Members of the early Christian Church "had all things common," as we read in the fourth chapter of Acts, but this system of rewards was eventually abandoned. The early settlers at Plymouth started out with a system of equal rewards, but likewise gave it up. In the vivid words of Governor William Bradford:

. . . At length, after much debate of things, the Gov (with the advise of the cheefest amongst them) gave way that they should set corne every man for his owne perticuler, and in that regard trust to them selves; in all other things to goe on in the generall way as before. . . . This had very good success for it made all hands very industrious, so as much more corne was planted then other waise would have bene by any means the Gov or any other could use, and saved him a great deall of trouble, and gave farr better contente. The women now wente willingly into the field, and tooke their litle-ons with them to set corne, which before would aledg weaknes, and inabilitie; whom to have compelled would have bene thought great tiranie and oppression.

In the nineteenth century several efforts were made in this country to build societies based on equal rewards. The communal society established by Robert Owen in New Harmony, Indiana, in 1825 lasted three years. The teachings of the French socialist Fourier were the basis of several short-lived Utopian settlements before the Civil War. A student of such enterprises, Albert Shaw, remarked in 1884, "In the last sixty years there have been hundreds of attempts at associative or communistic organizations in this country, all but a few of which failed in their very inception."

More recently the Soviet Union undertook to create an economy based on the credo "From each according to his ability, to each according to his needs." The criterion of "need" was quickly abandoned for the more easily administered criterion of "equality," and at the present time this is giving way to the more workable idea of "incentives."

The question of what is an equitable reward is a difficult one, not really in the economist's purview. But the question of what will get the goods produced *is* in his purview. I know of no economist, whether educated in Moscow, Paris, or New York, who would hold out any long-range hope for a society that insisted on equal rewards.

The consequences of equal rewards would be these:

Reduced production, as the motive for superior performance is ruled out.

Loss of initiative, as the pattern of one's life is determined for him by others.

Loss of variety, as standardization takes over.

Personal injustice, as genuine needs go unmet.

The additional and crucial feature in a system of equal rewards is that it requires a centrally directed economy. The free system will not produce equal rewards. Indeed, inequality of reward is the engine that powers the free economy. In a free and open system with a market economy, some individuals will be more gifted, more industrious, wiser, or luckier than others, and will have larger incomes. If one insists that rewards must be equal, he must thwart all these differences, whether they are the result of biology, initiative, or fortune. Since these forces are deep and powerful, it will take a tremendous effort to counteract them, in short, a centrally directed economy, with individual freedom sacrificed in the process.

To demand equal rewards is simply to demand a regimented society. The man who advocates equal rewards is saying that he considers individual freedom and responsibility to be ethically expendable.

The myth of equal shares has political potency as well as emotional appeal. Material goods are concentrated in relatively few hands. Any leveling process involves taking away from the few and giving to the many, an undertaking that becomes relatively easy in a society in which each man has a vote. Hence the politics of equal shares. If self-governing people are to avoid the error of equal shares, they must understand its pitfalls as well as its attractions.

The myth that considers equal rewards to be synonymous with fair treatment is erroneous, as has been shown. There is an opposite, rival myth: that fair treatment consists of having each person retain for himself the full amount that his effort, or his luck, or his heritage has put into his hands.

We should be wary of this one. The fact that a given myth is untenable does not validate the opposite view. The truth may lie somewhere between.

A word about the source of this myth. From the early years of our country until around the turn of this century, the competitive economy was not greatly challenged. Three fundamental rights were considered dominant: the right of the individual to own property, the right of the individual to engage in whatever form of economic activity he chose, and the right of free access to the market. It must be said immediately that such unrestricted rights were not and have never been fully granted. Certain property, such as military equipment, has almost always been publicly owned. Some enterprises, such as the narcotics trade, have long been outlawed. Access to the market has always been limited to some extent; there have long been regulations in the foreign exchange market and in futures trading, as on the Chicago Board of Trade. Like the completely regimented society, the completely free society has never existed. But in its broad outlines the free system long was dominant, and it continues so for many sectors of American life.

The market system — also known as "the price system," "the profit system," "the open system," "the free system," "capitalism," "free enterprise," "the competitive economy," and "laissez faire" — relied on the profit motive for its drive. Despite the fact that it is being challenged, it retains much vigor. The profit motive is the engine, price the steering wheel. The immense problems of supply are left to individuals, who follow the signals given by price. Whether a farmer produces hogs or broilers depends in part on the relative prices of the two. Whether a manufacturer produces black-and-white or color television depends on price. Whether a young man chooses to be a farmer, a coal miner, or an electrical worker depends, among other things, upon the relative returns. By differential returns, resources are shifted to the production of broilers, color television, and space technology.

Prices guide not only production but distribution as well. Whether milk should be consumed in its fluid state, churned into butter, pressed into cheese, evaporated, condensed, or dried, depends on relative prices. Whether steel is imported or exported depends on price. Whether laboring people move into Mississippi or California depends to a degree on wages, a form of price. The consumer chooses goods largely on the basis of price: turkey or ham, Chevrolet or Cadillac, metal or wood.

This system has built-in incentives for efficient production. The man who puts resources together most efficiently and who correctly anticipates the needs of the market is handsomely rewarded. If a man wrongly judges the needs of society or is wasteful in his use of resources, he suffers a loss. With this system the United States lifted itself, during a span of 150 years, from a wilderness to the most advanced industrial nation in the world.

The undeniable success of the system gave rise to the belief that a man has a right to earn and retain, without interference in any form, every dollar he can acquire. This belief embraces certain ethical judgments that are properly subject to question. If a man has inherited, through no effort of his own, the natural gift of superior managerial ability, is he entitled to all he can earn therewith? And if some other man is shortchanged at birth in terms of intelligence, health, or social position, is it appropriate therefore that he die, or live in poverty? Does the right to the product of one's own labor include the right to preferential treatment associated with institutional forms created through positions of power? Should a man who is in pursuit of his individual reward be absolved from the social and economic consequences his actions create for other people? Differences in incomes provide incentives, but wide differences in rewards are accompanied by envy and social unrest; how much should domestic tranquillity be jeopardized in the process of satisfying the acquisitive appetite? How much inducement should be offered to obtain that last increment of production? We speak of differences in income as being the necessary incentives for production; in order to provide incentives do we really need income differences as great as those that would be produced by a completely free economy?

These questions deserve more than a doctrinaire, categorical answer. In earlier days, when earning capacity was more dependent upon physical strength and manual skill, the top earners might have been able to make ten times the average income. But in our modern society, with the industrial complex now available and with the managerial tools now at hand, the earning capacity of the top man is perhaps a hundred or even a thousand times greater than the average. How big a salary could General Motors afford to pay to a president who would have such excellent judgment as to decide, correctly, whether or not to introduce a new line of cars? The difference between a good and a poor decision in such a matter would be measured in millions of dollars. Should this total difference accrue to the man who makes the right decision? A television entertainer may have an audience of thirty million people. Sandwiched between the acts may be an advertisement for razor blades. The best entertainer may be so superior to the next best as to be worth $100,000 extra to the advertiser. Should this full amount go to the better man? The Green Bay Packers figure that football player Donny Anderson is worth $600,000 to their team, and pay him that sum just to sign a contract. Should Anderson be able to keep the whole of this sum, undiminished by any income tax? Even the doctrinaire believer in full rewards must flinch at such a case.

If the evidence drives us away from the myth that equal rewards are just, as it does, we should not be driven to the opposite myth that justice lies in such inequality as arises from some uninhibited combination of power, fortune, skill, and enterprise.

By its laws the public has rejected both the myth of equal rewards and the myth of unrestrained economic freedom. The fact that we have rejected equal rewards is to be found in the observation that, despite substantial public intervention in economic life, about 75 percent of our economy is still private and essentially competitive, turning out rewards that are unequal. The fact that we have rejected the uninhibited operation of the market (sometimes called social Darwinism) is verified by the progressive income tax and public aid to people of low incomes.

For half a century or more our society has been moving in the direction of equal rewards, impelled by the idea that this is fair and equitable. As this tidal drift occurs, warning signals appear:

> There is danger that enterprisers, risk-takers, and job-creators, deprived of their incentives, may reduce their investments and their ventures, thereby slowing the rate of economic growth.
>
> There is danger that the less enterprising people, assured of their welfare payments, may lose some of their initiative and their willingness to work.
>
> There is danger that the central planning and the administrative machinery necessary to alter the pattern of rewards may rob the people of much of their freedom, their variety, their moral fiber, and their integrity.

The dangers in the last two possibilities seem greater than the danger in the first. Those who insist that equality of rewards is an appropriate objective point to the fact that the drive toward this goal has not thus far greatly inhibited the vigor and venturesomeness of the managerial class. They should look as well to the effect of this leveling process on the intended beneficiaries and to the effect on the quality of life.

There are thus two rival myths. The one favoring unrestrained competition with rewards grotesquely unequal is in rapid retreat. The other, the myth that rewards should be equal, is advancing steadily and poses the greater threat. Neither position is tenable, so a middle ground must be chosen. What shall it be? How steep the graduation of the income tax? What standard for public welfare? The answer may at first seem unsatisfactory, but it is honest. Any middle position is a compromise, resting on pragmatism and expediency rather than abstract reason. Hence no middle position has any logical anchoring. When challenged, as it will be, there is no rigorous logic with which it can be defended. Therefore, the degree of inequality in rewards will continue to be controversial and no compromise is likely to have permanence.

CHAPTER FOUR

The myths about money

How subtle the myths about money!
How elusive the facts, and how few!
If doubted, the fact becomes fable;
If believed, the myth becomes true!

Baron Rothschild, the famous French financier, was once heard to say that he knew of only two men who really understood money — an obscure clerk in the Bank of France and one of the directors of the Bank of England. "Unfortunately," he added, "they disagree."

That there should be widespread misunderstanding about money is not surprising. Despite its seeming simplicity, money is a very complicated subject. The institutional framework related to money has gradually been altered, particularly with the worldwide advent of central banking early in this century. As might be expected, public beliefs and attitudes have lagged behind these changes.

Most of the myths associated with money are the carryover of beliefs that were valid in an earlier day. They have their roots in mercantilism and are recognizable as the teachings of former monetary theorists. For the origin of these myths, we turn back the pages of history to a time when money was something more than a piece of paper currency or a checking account in the corner bank.

For many years money had utility in itself, apart from its use as a medium of exchange. Gold and silver were used as money, as were cattle, tobacco, beaver pelts, and many other commodities. Tobacco, beaver pelts, and other monies had demands of their own, to which, of course, were added whatever additional demands were derived from their use as money. Such monies were costly to produce. Their value fluctuated, separately from their monetary functions, in accordance with changes in their supplies and demands. But such changes tended to be moderate and these commodity monies had rather stable value. This kind of money we might call "full-bodied money." If the basis of the money system were to change from cattle to copper, for example, this change would not very much have affected the value of either the cattle or the copper.

This system was rather well understood by the people who used it. Myths were at a minimum. The theorists described the system in comprehensible terms. Money was real, not just a medium of exchange. It retained its ability to exchange for goods. It was a reasonably trustworthy store of value. For a king to tamper with such a currency was a grave betrayal of trust. The value of money was self-regulating, in need of little governmental supervision; its worth was determined by supply and demand, the same market forces that determined the values of other commodities.

With the passage of time, monetary institutions changed. The financial community came to realize that the most important attribute of money was confidence in it. If people trusted it, almost any kind of money would work. Paper money worked, so long as people believed in it. Cigarette money worked, as millions of Europeans discovered in the hectic days after World War II. There is in the South Pacific an island named Uap, whose money consists solely of stones called *fei*, many of them so large that they can scarcely be moved. The richest family on the island owes its wealth to the fact that it owns a huge stone which was accidentally lost off a raft while being brought to the island many years ago. For several generations this stone has been lying at the bottom of the sea; no living member of the family has ever seen it. But nobody questions that this is the richest family on the island.

Many changes followed from the discovery that confidence in the money was paramount. The banker learned to keep his gold locked in his vault and to issue paper claims against it. He learned that he could issue several times as many claims as he had gold because not everyone was likely to press his claim at the same time. So the fractional reserve system was born. Gold was ultimately withdrawn from circulation, so that the banking system could not be jeopardized by claims against the reserve. Central governments incurred debt, secured by bonds, and some of these bonds were used as reserves, against which currency was issued and loans were made. Thus part of the national debt was monetized. The resistance to the creation of money became the conscience of the public official, not the niggardliness of the mines. By degrees the money system changed. John Maynard Keynes, writing in 1930, prophetically described this shift:

Thus Gold, originally stationed in heaven with his consort, Silver, as Sun and Moon, having first doffed his sacred attributes and come to earth as an autocrat, may next descend to the sober status of a constitutional King with a Cabinet of Banks; and it may never be necessary to proclaim a Republic. But this is not yet — the evolution may be quite otherwise. The friends of Gold will have to be extremely wise and moderate if they are to avoid a Revolution.

These radical changes took place without the full understanding of the people. The banker, who kept a given amount of gold in his vault and issued many notes against it, took very few pains to explain this process. The public official, who now had the ability to increase the money supply so prodigiously as to reduce the value of the citizen's currency to a fraction of its earlier buying power, did not impress this capability on the public. The whole modern system of fractional reserves has about it such vulnerability to public apprehension that the responsible officials will strive to build confidence above all else — at the cost of frankness if necessary.

As so often is true, the body of belief changed less rapidly than the institutions. What had once been a valid belief became a myth, or a body of myths:

> That money has usefulness in and of itself.
>
> That it is somehow costly to produce and thus limited in amount.
>
> That it is a trustworthy store of value, safe from the threat of depreciation.

These things obviously are not true in the present institutional setting. The medium of exchange today is no longer full-bodied money; it is something distinctly different, something we may call credit money, or token money, or fiat money. It can be created in prodigious amounts, almost without cost, by the stroke of a pen. Its value can deteriorate; the buying power of the American dollar has declined 50 percent during the past forty years. Other currencies have depreciated far more. Whereas the value of a full-bodied money is largely self-regulating, this cannot be true of token money. Credit money, costing virtually nothing to produce, is of great value, but how can the supply of and demand for this money interact in a market setting so as to produce a currency of stable value? There is only one way to stabilize the value of a credit money, and this is with the monopoly power of the central government. States and local governments do not and cannot have this power, or chaos would reign.

The myth persists that credit money has intrinsic value and that it behaves economically like any other good. Here are some characteristic statements reflecting current misconceptions:

"The federal government doesn't have a single dollar which it did not first take from its citizens." On the contrary, the federal government, through the banking system, creates money by what amounts to a bookkeeping transaction.

"The government has to pay its debts, just as I do. It has to live within its means, just like a private citizen." Not so. The federal government can create money to pay its bills and can run a deficit every year from now until Doomsday. True, the value of the money might fall and the price level might rise. But the ability to create money is one of the distinguishing features of any modern national government.

"Maybe gold no longer circulates, but we have a gold reserve, and our money is based on gold." Not really. The base is small, less than $14 billion. The money based on it (currency plus demand deposits) is $175 billion. If we add "near money" (savings deposits plus U. S. bonds held by individuals and business), the total is in excess of half a trillion dollars. While there is a small gold base, our money is not redeemable in gold for domestic uses.

Beliefs about the inherent value of money occasionally get jolted. This happens at the Bureau of Engraving and Printing, where visitors can see the presses turning out huge sheets of bank notes as if they were so much advertising copy. At the Federal Reserve Banks, visitors can see bales of tattered old bank notes ground up like cornmeal. Why not? It costs almost nothing to replace them with fresh new ones. It is interesting to observe the human reaction to these two operations, as the idea penetrates that money does not have intrinsic value.

One thing that helps preserve the intrinsic value myth is the feeling that a full-bodied money has certain moral virtues attached to it. Something tells us that money without intrinsic value must be a very poor kind of money; it would be a form of moral decadence to believe in it. To create money out of thin air somehow evades the cost and pain that should be associated with the origin of something so valuable. Our intuitive feeling is that the process must be basically dishonest. It involves something-for-nothing, thereby calling for the same moral disapproval as gambling. If it was a betrayal of trust to tamper with a currency in years past, it must be so today.

It may indeed be a betrayal of trust, but it can be a very useful exercise. During the Great Depression, the monetary authorities were unable or unwilling to provide the amount of currency needed to maintain prices at something like their earlier level. From 1929 to 1932, the total amount of demand deposits and currency contracted by about $10 billion. What we needed then was a good number of skilled counterfeiters. If there had been ten thousand counterfeiters judiciously scattered around the country, each printing and distributing about a million dollars in bogus currency, the Great Depression might have been avoided. There were indeed some counterfeiters working during this period. They were duly run down and thrown in jail, a triumph of morality over economics.

One may wonder if it is wise to try to demythologize money. The myths inspire confidence in a country's currency, and this is hardly a bad thing. They permit the building of useful financial institutions. As suggested in Chapter One, myths regarding credit may be helpful. But these myths also have dangers in them. They are too far removed from present reality. They exclude the believer in them from meaningful participation in public policy concerning money and prices. They constitute a smoke screen of ignorance, behind which an unwise or unscrupulous public official can debauch the currency. The argument for preserving ignorance as a means of safeguarding the public interest is at best a dubious one. It would be better for people to be taught as much as they are able to understand about modern financial institutions; they would then be better guardians of the value of their money.

The inclination of many people is to regret the institutional changes that have shifted our unit of exchange from a full-bodied money to a credit currency. I do not share these feelings. Recognition that a money need not have intrinsic value relieved us of a difficult and costly task — digging precious metals out of the earth. The men and machines that might have been used for this purpose can now be used for the production of food, clothing, shelter, travel, education, health, recreation, and other useful goods and services.

True, the advent of credit money took the money-valuing forces away from those who dig and discover and placed them in the hands of those who officiate and administer. If one has a deep distrust of public officials, he perhaps would rather stake the value of his money on a chance stroke of the prospector's pick. To one who has considerable faith in the processes of representative government, the change has been an advance. I so consider it. We shall have to learn how to manage the new institutions related to money, but this is something worth learning.

Associated with the intrinsic value myth is a myth about the federal debt.

A citizen notes the $330 billion federal indebtedness, divides this by 200 million, our approximate present population, and comes out with a "per capita share of the federal debt" of about $1,600, which, if he is an average person, he figures he will have to pay in taxes. Or if the debt is not paid off, he figures his share of the interest on it at about $70 per year, which he will have to pay for the rest of his life. Thus he considers that he and his children are burdened with paying for our past and current extravagances. The average man, if he owns no government bonds, is surely in the situation described above, and no amount of argument can or should make him think otherwise. He is not dealing with a myth; so far as he himself is concerned, he is dealing with a fact.

The myth comes when we generalize from this man's situation to the economy as a whole. What is involved is a transfer of money within the group, not a net burden to the group, as shall now be explained.

It is widely believed that deficit financing can create benefits for the present generation that will somehow be extracted from our children and grandchildren. The great majority of Americans believe this and a number of our economists believe it. Nevertheless, it is a serious error.

Belief that deficit financing shifts the burden to the future fits into the thinking of many who advocate and many others who oppose the creation of debt. Some who feel little obligation to future generations favor deficit financing, believing that they can thus shift a cost to their children. A well-conditioned conscience feels no pain at such a plan. "What did posterity ever do for me?" aptly states this view. Other persons oppose debt because they feel moral constraints against burdening those yet unborn.

In order to dispel the myth about debt as a burden to our

children, we must see why it is that what holds true for an individual does not necessarily hold true for the group. Clearly, if an individual goes deeply into debt, he can raise his current consumption of goods, and if his debts are long-term he will bequeath them to his heirs. The heirs must then reduce their levels of living in order to retire the debt. Many of us know children who have had to cut their current spending to pay off their parents' debts. However, for this to happen to any significant degree on a nationwide basis is not possible. The goods and services a man consumes in the year 1968 must be produced in 1968 or in some earlier year; obviously they cannot be produced at some later time. The highways we build in a given year, the welfare services we provide, and the munitions we produce all must be supplied from resources used in that year or, of course, drawn from stocks made available in earlier years. The economist H. C. Adams states it clearly: "No father can eat the potatoes to be hoed by an unborn son."

Now, if an individual lifts his level of consumption by spending borrowed money, this increased consumption must either come from depriving someone else (which will be the case if the economy is at full employment) or from increased production (which may be the case if the economy is less than fully employed). *Within the borrowing year* there occurs a transfer or an increment of goods and services, accruing to the man who goes into debt. True enough! Now let the man die with his debt unpaid. Let his heirs receive their heritage in the form of a liability, and the heirs of the man from whom our borrower got his money receive their heritage in the form of an asset. To repay the debt, the borrower's heirs will deprive themselves of certain consumption, clearly enough, *during the repaying year*. And those who inherit the asset will have a transfer of goods and services made to them, *in that same year*.

67

In terms of micro-economics (the economics of the individual case) the situation seems clear; one generation, by its profligacy, has placed a burden upon the next. But in terms of macro-economics (the economics of the group) the case is quite different. There has been a shift in consumption levels from one person to another *within the borrowing year* and an offsetting shift *within the repaying year,* but no transfer between years. Both the micro and the macro analysis are needed. The error comes from assuming that what is true for a given individual is true for the group.

Now let us shift away from individual borrowing and repaying and consider the incurring of debt on the part of the federal government. The government spends, during the year, more than it obtains in taxes. To finance its deficit, it expresses its obligations in the form of bonds, some of them sold to the public. But sums spent by the government cannot create, during the deficit year, goods and services from the labor of children as yet unborn or from capital assets not yet fabricated! The goods and services provided during the deficit year must come from the production of that year (or from stocks produced in previous years). If the economy is fully employed, the deficit financing will simply cause inflation, leaving total production of goods and services unchanged. If the economy is less than fully employed, the added expenditure may engender a somewhat higher total level of output. In any case, there will be some transfer of goods and services *within the deficit year,* away from those individuals who buy the bonds and toward those in whose behalf the money is spent.

Let time pass. The bonds mature and are paid off. Those who held the bonds (or their heirs) receive an increment of goods and services; those who pay the taxes to retire the bonds experience a diminution in goods and services. There has been a transfer from one group to another *within the retirement year.* But there has been no transfer, on a national basis, *from one year to another,* or from one generation to another.

What can be said, in summary, that is both true and relevant?

(1) An individual can shift the time at which he consumes goods and services from one year to another because the rest of the economy conducts itself in so flexible a fashion as to accommodate itself to his decision.

(2) The economy generally must rely for its current consumption of goods and services on current production and stocks. It cannot commandeer goods as yet unproduced.

(3) One generation can confer benefits or handicaps on the one that follows. By wise investment, by prudently steering the ship of state, the fathers can bequeath a good heritage upon their children. Similarly, by allowing the industrial plant to run down or by allowing useful institutions to lapse, a bad legacy can be bequeathed.

(4) There is no way that a generation of people can confer goods or services upon their precedessors. They cannot do it by paying off their ancestors' debts.

Despite conservative antipathy to it, there is economic validity in the appraisal of the public debt that was current during the New Deal: "We owe it to ourselves."

The analysis here given assumes that the debt is held internally. If it is owed to a foreign nation the foregoing analysis does not hold. Then we do not "owe it to ourselves," and must export goods and services to obtain the foreign exchange with which to make payment.

There are plentiful and persuasive arguments against heavy deficit financing, as has been said. The chief one is that beyond some point deficit financing is inflationary, reducing the value of money, shrinking the buying power of savings, thereby levying upon the people what has been called the cruelest tax of all. But in an aggregative sense, deficit financing done domestically does not transfer purchasing power from one generation to another. To believe otherwise is to believe in a myth.

The real argument about federal debt stems from the fact that it accommodates and facilitates big government. The man we call a liberal favors it because he likes big government. The man we call a conservative opposes it because he opposes big government. Many of the contentions regarding federal debt have been contrived out of a desire either to facilitate or restrict the growth of the federal government.

There is yet another myth in the field of money that calls for examination. This one also concerns the public debt. According to the myth, there is some maximum level that the public debt can safely reach; if this level is exceeded it is alleged that the country will be plunged into bankruptcy. Like many illusions regarding money, this one arises from carrying into the public sector ideas that have validity for the individual. An individual has some maximum debt load that he can safely carry; the reasoning is that this must also be true for the country. The economist's job, presumably, is to identify the danger point at which the country would experience financial ruin.

This myth traces back to the 1930's when the federal debt began to mushroom. A maximum debt tolerance, widely quoted at the time, was $40 billion. With the debt now eight times this large and the country thriving, we might well be cautious in announcing a maximum limit for the national debt.

The myth of a safe maximum indebtedness arises each time the Congress debates the statutory debt limit. Of all the legislative operations undertaken by the Congress, this is probably the most ludicrous. The Congress, in a sanctimonious gesture, salutes the idea of fiscal responsibility; it establishes a debt limit. It then votes for appropriations clearly violating the limit it has set. When the bills come due and it is clear that the limit must be raised, there is a new debate, equally solemn. But the Congress finally bails itself out by lifting the debt ceiling, setting a new, higher, and presumably wiser limit.

The difficulties involved in carrying the national debt are essentially two. One is the problem of raising some $14 billion from one set of people, the taxpayers, and paying out this $14 billion, in interest, to another set of people, the bondholders. There is considerable overlap between the two groups. While this increases the role of government in the collection and disbursement of money, it simply involves a transfer of funds and, apart from the relatively minor costs of administration, leaves the country as a whole neither better nor worse off. Thirteen billion dollars is less than 2 percent of the gross national product — on a relative basis not a prodigious amount. The other problem is management of the debt, "rolling over" a substantial share of it each year, that is, issuing new bonds as old ones are paid off, exercising proper concern for capital markets and interest rates. This is a sizable but not an impossible job. It would be extremely difficult to demonstrate that the country is close to its economic capacity in performance of these two tasks.

Of all the criteria for public financing, the idea of a dollar limit on the national debt is the poorest. Ours is a growing economy; if there were a proper figure for the federal debt for a given year, it would be outmoded the following year. The most significant thing about the federal debt is that a large part of it has now been monetized; that is, it has become the basis for expanding the amount of money in circulation. Its magni-

71

tude and its changing dimensions affect the volume of currency and credit and thus the value of the dollar and the level of economic activity.

All right, we will reject a fixed maximum level of indebtedness as a basis for judging the level of federal taxation and spending. What, then, are the possible policy objectives? In Table III various objectives are listed in order according to their effect on the price level, running from the most deflationary to the most inflationary.

TABLE III

Taxing and Spending: Objectives and Consequences

	Objectives	Proposed action	Effect on price level
(1)	Moral rectitude	"Pay off the debt"	Sharp deflation
(2)	Fiscal account-ability	"Balance the budget every year"	Deflation, instability
(3)	Minimize economic fluctuations	"Balance the budget over the business cycle"	Deflation
(4)	Provide an honest dollar	"Let the debt change at whatever rate or in whatever direction is needed to achieve relatively stable prices"	General stability
(5)	Promote economic growth	"Engage in deficit financing to achieve full employment"	Moderate inflation
(6)	Pour out public money	"Deficit financing as a way of life"	Sharp inflation

With our present monetary institutions, to pay off the national debt would be to shrink the basis for our credit and currency. With a reduced supply of money, prices would fall, investment would be reduced, employment would decline, and we would be plunged into a sharp deflation.

To balance the budget either annually or over a given cycle would, unless new monetary institutions were developed, result in a failure to provide the increasing amount of money required to accommodate the needs of a growing economy.

Taxing and spending policies designed to produce a generally stable price level would maximize the likelihood that the economy could achieve a fairly good overall performance with a modest level of government intervention. This is the policy I prefer.

To incur large and numerous deficits in an effort to push the economy constantly toward full employment would result in running an inflationary fever.

To throw all caution to the winds and accept deficit financing as a way of life, based on the idea that it is more popular to create and distribute money than to extract it from the people in the form of taxes, would be the ultimate in irresponsibility. Inflation would run rampant as it has in every country that has followed such a course. Brazil and Argentina are cases in point.

The administrations of Eisenhower, Kennedy, and Johnson have worked toward three goals: economic growth, a stable price level, and avoidance of recessions. Clearly, no one of the cited objectives is sufficient in itself. The emphasis has shifted over time; during the first half of the sixties there was more concern about promoting economic growth and less about preventing inflation. There are long arguments as to the appropriateness and the compatibility of the three goals: growth, stability, and a dollar of constant value. In a broad sense I believe the goals are mutually reinforcing. Deficit financing, judiciously used, is a legitimate tool in achieving any or all of them. To ask what a safe dollar limit for the national debt would be is to ask the wrong question. The question is based on the myth that such a figure exists.

Most reactions go too far. There has been a reaction against the old myths about money. In the world of practical affairs, the best way to overcome a myth is not by attacking it head-on, but rather by setting up a rival myth. Thus a new family of myths has arisen. In their extreme form these new myths are:

> That spending is a virtue and that saving is wicked.
>
> That since the government can create money, government goods and services do not really cost anything.
>
> That government activities are not really costly, and that therefore they need not be scrutinized carefully as to their usefulness.
>
> That since a big federal debt does not really place a burden on our children, we can in good conscience run any size deficit we wish.
>
> That inflation, a by-product of excessive spending, is in fact economically beneficial.

Advocates of these new myths are fond of quoting John Maynard Keynes, who overthrew the beliefs about hard money and designed the new economics. But they do not read their master well. Keynes praised the virtue of profit and preached the perils of inflation. He said, "There is no subtler, no surer means of overturning the existing basis of a society than to debauch the currency."

A part of the new mythology is the belief that we spend far too little of our money on government programs, that there is something in our system that results in private luxury and public squalor. In my opinion, the opposite argument has

74

equal justification. The demand for government services is similar to the demand for food on the part of a large group that sits down to dinner and agrees to prorate the bill. If a man knows that the cost of the meal will be shared equally among the group, he is likely to order an expensive meal. He could save himself only a few pennies by ordering hamburger. Similarly, the demand for government services is amplified by the concentration of benefits and the dispersion of costs.

The new myths about money are as erroneous as the old ones, and are probably more dangerous. Saving is still the means by which economic growth is achieved, as we shall see in Chapter Seventeen. To refrain from consuming one's whole product, to save some of it and then invest it in the building of machines and the training of men—this is how economic development occurs.

Government services are not costless, even though they are purchased with credit money. They require the labor of men and the use of machines. If labor and capital are used for the production of less needed goods, they cannot be used to produce things more needed. This is still a vital principle. A federal debt of inflationary proportions will shrink the value of every savings bond, every life insurance policy, every pension, every fixed income. Inflation drives capital out of the country and distorts the pattern of investment. It rewards the speculator and it breeds a corrosive cynicism about government, contracts, and financial institutions.

Perhaps the best way to examine these new myths is to look at the experiences of the countries that have embraced them with the most enthusiasm. These have generally been the less-developed countries, where economic growth is most ardently desired, where taxes are hardest to raise, and where official resistance to the desire for public spending has been weakest. These countries have experienced marked inflation.

TABLE IV

Index Numbers of Wholesale Prices in 58 Countries, for the Year 1965 or 1964 (1958 = 100)

Country	Index	Country	Index
Brazil	1919	Iraq*	114
Argentina	767	United Arab Republic	113
Chile	429	Zambia	113
Korea, Republic of	221	Ecuador	112
Colombia	201	Italy	112
Turkey	154	Ivory Coast*	112
India	145	Norway	112
Gabon	144	Iran	111
Israel	144	Netherlands	111
China (Taiwan)	140	New Zealand	111
Central African		Belgium	110
Republic*	138	Canada	110
Morocco	137	Switzerland	109
Philippines	137	Australia	108
Viet Nam, Republic of	131	Portugal	108
Spain	130	South Africa	108
Yugoslavia	129	Germany, Federal	
Senegal	128	Republic of	107
Tunisia	126	United Kingdom	107
Finland	124	Rhodesia, Southern	106
Venezuela	122	Syria*	105
France	121	Costa Rica	104
Sweden	120	Japan	104
Greece	119	United States	102
Austria	118	Guatemala	101
Pakistan	118	Puerto Rico	101
Dominican Republic	117	Ethiopia	99
Ireland	117	El Salvador	97
Mexico	117	Thailand	96
Denmark	115	Burma*	89

Source: "Index Numbers of Wholesale Prices," *United Nations Monthly Bulletin of Statistics,* July 1966, pp. 134–145.
* 1964.

Table IV is a measure of the rate of inflation in 58 countries, all those for which statistics are available, shown in index numbers for the year 1965 or 1964, using 1958 as a base. Prices, it will be noted, rose in all but four of the 58 countries.

Price data are available for various countries for earlier periods. Table V shows the average annual percentage changes in the price level for 39 countries during a time long past, 1910 to 1939, a time of general monetary conservatism, when most countries were operating under the old myths. These figures are contrasted with the average annual percent changes during 1958 to 1964, a recent period of widespread deficit financing, when most countries were operating under the new myths. These 39 countries include all those for which price data are available for both periods. For 26 of the 39 countries, price behavior was more inflationary under the new myths than under the old, despite the fact that the 1958–64 period was one of relative peace and should therefore have been expected to show general price stability.

Clearly, the new myths have provided an institutional and psychological setting in which the value of the currencies is subject to serious erosion. If the retreat of the old myths is to prove a real blessing, we must campaign against the new myths that threaten to replace them.

The known and reputable body of theory on money, credit, and prices is a narrow piece of high ground, flanked on one side by the jungle of ancient myth and on the other by a dream world. Something like this is true for many of the areas of economics. But for money, the high ground is narrower, the mythical world larger, and the denizens thereof wilder. In Chapter Fourteen, an effort is made to sketch out this high ground.

TABLE V

Average Yearly Percentage Change in the Price Level, 39 Countries

	1910 to 1939		1958 to 1964
Brazil	−1.0		94.0
Argentina	−.7		65.0
Chile	5.6		21.5
Korea, Republic of	4.6		8.2
Peru	1.8		8.2
China	12.5	(Taiwan)	7.2
Turkey	−1.6		7.2
Palestine	0.0	(Israel	6.2
Philippines	.4		4.7
India	−2.6		3.2
France	2.3		2.8
Spain	3.9		2.3
Venezuela	−2.3		2.3
Finland	1.6		1.7
Greece	2.5		1.7
Mexico	1.2		1.7
Sweden	1.2		1.7
Austria	−.6		1.3
Costa Rica	1.0		1.3
Denmark	1.8		1.3
Yugoslavia	−1.0		1.3
Canada	−1.3		1.2
Ecuador	−1.7		1.2
Ireland	2.5		1.0
Italy	1.6		1.0
Switzerland	−1.4		1.0
New Zealand	1.1		.8
Belgium	−1.4		.7
Germany	−1.7	(Federal Republic of)	.7
Iran	4.0		.7
Norway	1.2		.7
Japan	4.1		.5
Portugal	.5		.5
South Africa	−.1		.5
Australia	−.4		.3
United Kingdom	.3		.3
Netherlands	−2.1		.2
United States	−1.1		0.0
Thailand	8.0		−.2

Sources: 1910–39: "Wholesale Prices, Index Numbers," *Statistical Yearbook, 1949–50,* United Nations, New York, 1950, pp. 387–399; and 1958–64: "Index Numbers of Wholesale Prices," *United Nations Monthly Bulletin of Statistics,* Vol. XIX, No. 7, United Nations, New York, 1965, pp. 130–141.

CHAPTER FIVE

The myth that what works for the individual will work for the group (and vice versa)

If Joe does what seems best for him,
What effect has this on Jim?
If Joe and Jim collaborate,
What effect has this on Nate?

In 1776 Adam Smith, that canny Scot, wrote this sentence into his *Inquiry into the Nature and Causes of the Wealth of Nations:* "What is prudence in the conduct of every private family, can scarcely be folly in that of a great kingdom." This concept has become distilled in a myth which holds that whatever is good for the individual is good for the group. Believers in freedom, advocating the least possible restraint on individual decision-making, contend that such freedom will be wisely used by the individual and will result in decisions that are good for the group.

But Smith also understood that the interests of the individual and the state could diverge. One of the duties of the sovereign, he said, was "that of protecting, as far as possible, every member of the society from the injustice or oppression of every other member of it."

The relationship of the individual to the group is a complex matter, not well adapted to generalization and not well described by myths. To assume that there is invariably an identity of interest between the individual and the group is to overlook much evidence to the contrary. On the other hand, to contend that there is always a conflict is to set the stage for advocating either anarchy or regimentation. There is no simple way to describe the directional flow of good and nongood between individual and group.

Almost by intuition one assumes an association between what he finds good in his own situation and what he presumes to be good for the whole society. The process has compelling support in the human heart. Who would not be buoyed up by the belief that his vocational calling, his aspirations, and his judgments are not only appropriate to him but are in the public interest? Every business executive wants to think that what is good for his company is also good for America. Every worker wants to think that the objectives of the laboring man are in keeping with the good of the country. And every farmer wants to believe that if he is doing well the country will be prosperous. The desire to believe this myth is very deep.

Unlike most others in this book, this particular myth has in it far more truth than error. We saw in Chapter Two and will see again in Chapter Nine that compatibility between the interest of the individual and the group is a common thing. But while belief in the identity of individual and group interests is perfectly valid in the great majority of cases, it can lead us into deep error and, in fact, often does so. Logicians have a name for this error. They call it "the fallacy of composition."

We have already had a strong hint, in the previous chapter, that what works for the individual may not work for the group. We saw that public finance is basically different from private finance. We saw that an individual can borrow, lift his level of living, and present the bill to his heirs. But if everybody was to attempt this at once, the efforts would cancel themselves out.

The most noteworthy illustration of the conflict between individual and group interest occurs in respect to saving. Most of us were brought up to believe that individual saving is a good thing. "A penny saved is a penny earned," said Ben Franklin. One recalls the famous equations of Charles Dickens' Mr. Micawber: "Income 20 pounds, outgo 19 pounds, 19 shillings and 6 pence; result: happiness. Income 20 pounds, outgo 20 pounds, 6 pence; result: trouble."

This is all well enough if the economy is booming along and the savings get invested. But suppose there is some slack, some unemployment, some unused manufacturing capacity, some considerable amount of savings already idle in the bank vaults. Then the effort on the part of individuals to save can lead to tragic consequences for the economy. If, in such a situation, people were to decide to save, and so to spend less than they take in, the savings would accumulate unspent, there would be less spending the next time around and still less the next until the economy would finally stagnate. The effort to save more would, in fact, result in less actual saving, and the course that seemed wise to the individuals would turn out to be tragic for the group. Professor Paul Samuelson has called this the "paradox of thrift"; private prudence becomes social folly.

This is exactly what happened during the Great Depression. People were mistakenly urged to tighten their belts and save more in order to restore prosperity. Authorities, notably John Maynard Keynes, understood that the adage about saving was then a myth; their counsel was to spend, not to save. This advice ran contrary to past experience, was in opposition to the Puritan ethic, and was in conflict with the then received economic doctrine. But it was right, *for that time*. It is not right during generally good times, when saving and investment is the proper course. Some of those who had correctly advocated spending during the Depression tried to make spending into a universal principle, applicable to all phases of the business cycle. As we have seen, this was another error.

The myth that what will work for the individual will work for the group is also to be found in agriculture. The individual farmer finds it good to adopt new, efficient practices. He gets his cost per bushel down and increases his production. Other things equal, his income rises. But while one farmer is doing this, the others are by no means idle. They also adopt the new techniques and increase output. Consumers, having already largely satisfied their food needs, will pay relatively little for this added output. Prices fall. Thus an action which, other things equal, would help the net income of an individual farmer, may, if generally adopted, turn out (in the short run) to reduce the incomes of farmers as a group. In the long run, of course, some farmers would take city jobs where they would produce industrial products, housing, and a variety of services. Thus the situation would be improved for the whole economy, including the farmers.

Here are a few more examples of how a thing which works for the individual may not work if all individuals undertake it:

During a wartime shortage of goods, a hoarder may improve his own situation by stocking up on a scarce article. But if all attempt to do so, the result is injurious.

The first grocery stores to issue trading stamps gained an advantage thereby. But when practically all stores were issuing stamps they became little more than a nuisance.

If a man stands up at a football game he can see the play better; if everyone stands up the average fan cannot see as well as before.

In the old days, before Federal Deposit Insurance, a man might sense that his bank was in trouble and withdraw his savings, thinking thereby to improve his situation. But he might thus precipitate a run on the bank, forcing it to close its doors to the injury of many including himself.

Any effort to universalize the idea that what is good for the individual is good for the group will run into these obvious contradictions. As an all-embracing concept the myth is untenable.

These departures from the compatibility of individual and group benefits became highly visible during the Great Depression, but, as is often the case, the reaction went too far. The idea arose that the basic relationship between the individual and the group was one of conflict rather than compatibility. The group interest was thought to supersede the individual interest, to which it was now believed to be opposed. It was now considered appropriate, therefore, that the group coerce the individual throughout a wide range of areas. These ideas were forcefully put and given general application in private as well as public life. They became themselves a myth, the opposite of the one just discussed. It is interesting, and perhaps indicative of the present strong belief in group action, that those who studied and labeled the error which states that the individual and the group interest are identical have failed to develop a label for the error which assumes that individual and group interests are opposed.

Here is a list of some public programs that stem from the new belief that individual and group interests are opposed and that individuals should be coerced into actions deemed to be in the interest of the group:

Saving: Through various social security programs, decisions on saving have been taken out of the hands of individuals, who are now required to conform to group judgments.

Agriculture: Through acreage limitations, decisions on land use have been transferred from individual farmers to Washington officials.

Health: Through Medicare, people who are able to meet their own health needs and who are able and willing to carry private insurance are nevertheless required to participate in the group program.

Power: Development of power sites is increasingly a matter for public rather than private decisions, stemming from the belief that private decisions on these matters will be contrary to the best interests of the group.

Housing: Rent subsidies, public housing, urban redevelopment, and zoning ordinances all attest the subordination of individual to group decisions in the housing area.

As was said earlier, the true relationship of the individual to the group is complex. It is a suitable subject for philosophical reflection, sociological research, economic experimentation, and political innovation. To try to describe it in terms of universals is to oversimplify beyond tolerable bounds. To declare individual and group interests to be always compatible is a myth. To describe them as basically opposed is likewise a myth, doubtless a more dangerous one. In any case, such divergence as may exist between the interest of the individual and the interest of the group is less in the long run than it is in the short run. No ready-made answer will substitute for the diligent examination of this relationship, case by case.

CHAPTER SIX

The myth that if the government does it, it's good (or bad)

"It's government-run; we voted for it.
So why complain and why deplore it?"

"But is it better, is it wiser
To give the job to a centralizer?"

This chapter and the next two deal at least as much with political as with economic mythology. I have been unable, in these three chapters, to separate political science from economics. This is not surprising; our discipline was called "political economy" before it was called "economics," and the meticulous manner in which the two fields are often bounded undoubtedly has about it a good deal of artificiality. For the next three chapters, then, the distinctions are consciously blurred. It is necessary to proceed in this fashion to handle the economic content in a reasonably realistic manner.

On the next page is a simplified diagram developed by the logician John Venn in 1880. Let one circle represent economics and the other politics. The area in which they overlap takes on the attributes of both disciplines; to try to separate them would be presumptuous. The next three chapters concern this area of overlap.

A great issue of our time is the degree to which decision-making should be an individual, as contrasted with a governmental, responsibility. We have already seen that many of the

85

myths have implicit in them some judgments on this question, and that there are no easy answers. Unfortunately, what the average person really wants is a ready-made criterion by which

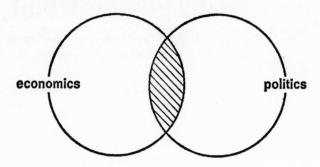

any economic proposal may be judged. He wants instant appraisal, just as he wants instant coffee. Since almost every current proposal will have as a major element the issue of individual versus governmental responsibility, the simplest thing for this citizen to do is to take, in advance, a position for or against government participation in economic life. Once he has made this single decision, all else can follow for him, quickly and without much study.

Suppose a man decides that government participation in economic decision-making is a good thing. He hears of some proposal and needs ask only one question: "Does it mean more governmental activity, or does it mean less?" If it means more, he's for it. If it means less, he's against it. Reverse this for the rival view.

These positions are stereotyped, of course, and they come from stereotyped views of the individual, of his institutions, and of his government. Here are the rival positions in some detail:

(1) *The position in favor of government action.*

The individual, as seen by proponents of government action, is inclined to do things contrary to the public interest. In part this inclination is thought to be congenital, in part the result of having been brought up in a flawed institutional setting. The remedies are thought to be two:

(a) Change the institutions so as to improve the likelihood that the individual will conduct himself, voluntarily, in a manner better suited to the group, and

(b) Require individual deportment appropriate to group objectives, in addition to such modified behavior as may be achieved through environmental change.

Government is viewed as a superior means of achieving the purposes of the group. This is primarily because in government there is one vote per person; through government the humble people are given as much consideration as the exalted. By contrast, in competitive private life the well-to-do person may be a hundred times as powerful as the poor man. But there is nothing to fear from government, say the advocates of centralized decision-making, because with our representative system the government and the people are really one and the people need not fear themselves.

(2) *The position against government action.*

People who oppose government action consider individual fulfillment to be the major goal, more worthy than the achievement of some group objective. They doubt that group objectives can be spelled out in a manner suitable to our many citizens, and they are reluctant in any case to delegate this task to a public official. They look on diversity with greater approval, and on conformity with more misgivings, than do the pro-government people. They have a high regard for the ability of the individual to make wise decisions if he has the necessary information, and they are anxious to provide him with the facts.

These people consider the market a generally good institution, serving the citizenry rather well. It may be in need of some modification and some improvement, but such changes, they believe, should be undertaken for the purpose of strengthening the market rather than substituting something else for it. Government, according to these people, is an instrument of power and, as such, suspect. Lord Acton is quoted: "Power tends to corrupt, and absolute power corrupts absolutely." Those who oppose government action are reluctant to subject the individual to the decision of a majority of his fellows. Governments, set up to protect the general interest from the special interest, are believed to do the exact opposite. Politically powerful groups have their lobbies and achieve their objectives, say these advocates of freedom; the politically weak do not. Individualists believe that disadvantaged groups have a better chance to improve their situation through the competitive system than they do through public programs.

Thus, the rival positions. They appeal more to emotion than to reason. The arguments are easy to understand and hard to refute. They overgeneralize. They have enough truth to make them convincing and enough falsehood to make them dangerous. All of them attack; none defends or explains. "The best defense is a good offense" has as much validity in this field as in any other. Here are the major and more respectable arguments spawned by the rival positions:

Pro-government clichés:

"Private interests are strong, selfish, and harmful. The only way they can be checked is by strong government action."

"We can move faster when action is unified."

"Important basic economic and social needs go unmet unless the government takes them on."

"The market system may have been all right for an earlier day, but modern society is too complex for it to function satisfactorily."

"We have learned that centralized decision-making is the way to win a war; it is also the way to achieve peacetime objectives."

Anti-government clichés:

"A man will work harder for himself than for somebody else."

"Individual cases are too complex to be handled properly in a standardized government program."

"Government programs would rob the society of its diversity."

"We have succeeded well as a private, competitive economy; why give this up for something new and untried?"

"To centralize decision-making would be to convert us to the pattern of our Communist rivals; we can't succeed with their system."

The citizen occasionally grows weary of the strife and wishes it would cease. But it will not. The issue cannot be adjourned. Stripped of showmanship, clichés, and vote-seeking, the issue is central. It divides the world, not just the United States.

What can we say of these two opposed beliefs? We can say that each of them, if believed in by the people, will validate itself and prove true. If either of them lacks popular support, it will be proven false.

In the United States there has long been a body of belief which holds that the market economy is generally able to allocate resources, move commodities through the channels of trade, and guide the processes of consumption. This belief has led to the development of an economy which has given us the highest level of living and the greatest degree of individual freedom to be found anywhere in the world. But this performance is not automatic. It rests on the belief that the market can indeed perform these functions. The performance will be forthcoming so long as this belief holds — and no longer. If we lose confidence in the individual and in the competitive market, if we are no longer willing to rely on them, then the system based on individual responsibility loses its capacity to function well, just as a football team that has lost confidence in itself loses the ability to win. If believed in, the myth — it may be so characterized — is self-validating and immensely useful; if disbelieved, it is useless. The doubters, having destroyed the myth, would then be able to say, "I told you so."

In similar fashion, the idea that an economy can be centrally directed by government is a myth capable of validation. The successful functioning of such a society is dependent on the acceptance of it as a workable, desirable system. In the

Soviet Union, where the myth is accepted, the system operates, in its own fashion. If the belief should ever become widespread there that the centrally directed system cannot function satisfactorily, the system would fail.

Almost any economic system will function, *if accepted*. That is, it will provide, in greater or lesser amount, the necessities of life, it will provide the citizen with a role that he will come to accept, and it will inspire considerable loyalty.

I have lived in various institutional settings with various economic systems, all of which appeared to work: a midwestern family-farming community, strongly committed to individual enterprise; a college town, heavily dependent upon a state university; and Washington, D. C., a cosmopolitan city dominated by the federal government. I have studied at first hand the industrial complex of the United States, the traditional rural economy of the Malay Peninsula, and the peasant agriculture of Southern France. Though vastly different, all of these seem to be working — in the sense that they supply their people with reasonably adequate quantities of goods and services, as judged by the people themselves, and they appear to be accepted by those who participate therein.

I have also seen economies that appear not to be performing satisfactorily and are, therefore, in the process of change: the economy of the Negro community in much of the United States, and the feudalistic economy in parts of Latin America.

Clearly, these various economies have ranged widely in the degree of responsibility they have placed on the individual and on the government. And their performance, as measured by their output and by their acceptance, has also varied.

Is there another, perhaps a more important criterion for judging these economies? I think so. Let us examine the effect of the system on the quality and character of the people. Here, perhaps the educator and the man of letters are better able to comment than the economist. The people produced by these systems range all the way from the totally submissive "dull driven cattle" cited by Longfellow to W. E. Henley's complete individualist who cries that he is the master of his fate and the captain of his soul. Not very attractive fellows, either the submissive subject or the ungovernable rebel. To be preferred, I think, are people whom James Conant describes as having "a small, hard core of common agreement, surrounded by a rich variety of individual differences."

The two myths, one advocating and one opposing strong government participation in economic affairs, go back at least to the time of Plato. Neither one in its pure form seems fully acceptable to most societies, at least for long. Economic systems seem to trend gradually toward one or the other of the extremes. As the extreme of individual decision-making is approached, license and disorder cause a shift toward stronger government. After a sustained drift toward central government, the infringement of individual liberty becomes intolerable and reaction occurs. The United States has now finished nearly two hundred years of history as a nation. The first hundred saw a strong bent toward individual responsibility; the second hundred a drift toward strong central government. Thus do the two great myths react on one another; as the society moves in the direction of one of these myths, past some optimum point, that myth grows weak and the other gains strength. They can be expected to continue to coexist, and to have a long, contentious life.

If a man is to participate in the public arena, by thought, word, or deed, he will have to come to some kind of terms with these myths. Abraham Lincoln's formula comes to mind: "The legitimate task of government is to do those things which the individuals cannot themselves do, or cannot so well do, in their individual and separate capacities. In all other things, government ought not to interfere." The merit of this view is that it places the individual and his needs at the center of interest. His individual fulfillment is the goal. Private or public actions are considered as alternative means to this goal, not as ends in themselves. As regards the government's role in economic life, the position is pragmatic, not doctrinaire. While this approach may not satisfy either of the contending camps, it does help people to develop and grow in directions that they themselves feel to be good.

This view is clearly set forth by Richard Cornuelle in his recent book *Reclaiming the American Dream*. Cornuelle makes a powerful plea for voluntary action by what he calls "the independent sector," the nongovernmental groups that associate themselves for common causes: the service clubs, the churches, the charitable foundations, the labor unions, the trade associations, and many others. By voluntary action of the independent sector, Cornuelle says, we could avoid both the negativism of the anti-government group and the weakened individual responsibility which results from too much government.

CHAPTER SEVEN

The myth
of heroes
and villains

Find a hero, cheer him proudly,
All good things to him we owe!
Name a villain, hiss him loudly,
Blame on him all worldly woe!

The great myths of literature are liberally supplied with heroes
and villains. In fact, the essence of mythology is the personifi-
cation of events. When the volcano erupted, Vulcan was at
work; when the waves rose, Poseidon was troubled; if events
went against a man, it was because some god had thwarted
him.

One of the great myths of economics is the personifica-
tion of hopes and problems, the explanation of events in terms
of individual acts. This myth has immense appeal: It simplifies
complex matters, permits instantaneous appraisal of current
proposals, and provides an outlet for the human desire to extol
virtue and castigate villainy.

The utility of instant identification will be plain to anyone
who has watched a television Western. The audience wants to
know whom to pull for and whom to be against, so heroes
wear white hats or ride white horses, and the villains scowl or
leer. One can switch on the set in the middle of a program and
be current as to the plot in a moment.

So with the economic myths. Should the citizen favor some

proposal? This is not a difficult matter. He identifies his hero and notes where the hero stands on the question; if the hero is for it, the citizen feels safe in supporting it. More likely, the citizen decides what he himself is for, and attaches the hero's label to any public figure who concurs. These expressions of the myth are what we might call its positive form. In the negative form the citizen identifies a villain and takes an opposite position. Or he decides what he is for and labels as villainous anyone who opposes his view.

Heroes and villains can be individual persons, political parties, vocational groups, or causes. Among the individual heroes there is the elder-statesman type, the man of action, the rough-hewn man of the people, or the man of principle. Among the villains there is the pawn of the vested interest, the unscrupulous man, the expedient man, and the man who is simply uninformed. Men in public life become type-cast. The man who accidentally acquires a hero's billing is fortunate indeed; the man who has the misfortune to be designated a villain can spend the rest of his life trying to detach the label.

How accurate are these labels? Not very accurate, obviously. Most men and most organized groups of men are too complex to be accurately tabbed as villainous or heroic.

What caused the Great Depression? The myth says that Herbert Hoover was responsible, though I have counted 42 additional explanations in the literature of the 1930's, put forward by responsible people, for that complex event.

Why does the farm population keep declining? The myth says that the farmers are being driven off their farms by the Secretary of Agriculture — this despite the documented fact that the technological revolution is responsible.

What causes wages to rise? The myth delegates sole responsibility to the labor unions, despite the fact that the trend began long before there were any unions and despite the fact that wages rise in nonunionized as well as in unionized industries and plants.

Who is for fiscal responsibility? The Republicans, says the myth, though the Grand Old Party can count some great spenders among its number. Who is for the common man? The Democrats, says the myth, despite the fact that a large sector of that party represents the privileged part of society.

Who are the heroes saluted by those of us who regard ourselves as liberals? Among others, the myth lists Jefferson, Jackson, and Franklin Roosevelt, though certainly Jefferson and perhaps also Jackson would be ill at ease with programs now offered under the liberal label. Who are the heroes recognized by those of us who consider ourselves conservatives? Among others, Hamilton, Lincoln, and Robert Taft, though Lincoln certainly frightened some of the conservatives of his time.

If a man is cast as a hero it does not follow that he need be heroic in every act. Greek mythology reveals whim and self-indulgence on the part of its heroes and occasional acts of greatness on the part of its villains. This helped to make them credible. Modern heroes and villains of economic myth show like attributes. Franklin Roosevelt indulged his whims, as the historian Arthur Schlesinger tells us, and showed remarkable ambivalence in simultaneously pursuing opposed objectives. And still within his lifetime Herbert Hoover was partially converted from villain to hero.

Certain causes come to be identified in economic mythology as heroic: the fight against monopoly, the fight against inflation, the fight for labor. Another is the fight for pure food, exemplified in the "cranberry crisis" of 1959, when the Department of Health, Education and Welfare prohibited the sale of berries containing such infinitesimal quantities of herbicide that someone calculated a person would have to consume thirteen tons of them in order to experience injury.

Other causes become identified as villainous. The desire of farmers to employ seasonal workers younger than the legal minimum age is one. Another is the private development of hydroelectric sites.

Sometimes a cause will shift from one category to another. Protecting American industry from foreign imports, once a heroic action, is now villainous. The cause of agriculture was once heroic, but the city man, with his far greater number of votes, finds the merit of his cause increasing relative to that of his country cousin.

Many of us like to think of ourselves as analytical. We have some awareness of the intricacy of events, the complexity of the individual human being, and the role of chance in public affairs. We are repelled by oversimplification, by carefully built-up heroes, and by the sacrificial role imposed on those labeled as villains. But we have to remind ourselves that we are a nation of nearly 200 million people, served by 535 senators and congressmen, now spending some $135 billion in federal money on thousands of different programs. It is simply not possible for even a thoughtful individual to weigh fully and fairly the qualifications of all these people, or the merits of all these programs. Despite the desire for objective analysis, some simplification becomes a practical necessity. And the public as a whole is quite disposed to join in this process. Despite our boasted commitment to democratic principles, we are prone to lift up a leader, attribute superior virtue to him, and accord him an exalted and heroic position. And we feel a similar need to personalize our troubles, to find a scapegoat, to create a villain.

The adulation of heroes would come a little harder to the public if they could somehow be present in the smoke-filled room where the image of the hero is consciously built up. And the villain might call forth admiration instead of disapproval if the public could witness him courageously taking responsibility for some necessary but unpopular action, while the hero runs for cover. The propagation, care, and feeding of heroes and villains is a well-developed branch of political husbandry.

Of course there are some authentic heroes and some genuine villains, and these are often discovered. The country's leaders do indeed make decisions that have far-reaching consequences, for good and ill. It is appropriate for the people to try to take the measure of their leaders, and to appraise their acts. The problem comes with oversimplification, to which process the leader himself is often a party. He tries to receive credit for more than he really deserves. It is a matter of poetic justice, perhaps, that he also then be charged with responsibility for more than his share of the things that go wrong.

Demythologizing economics is a difficult task. A teacher of the subject may spend a full class period with thirty students, analyzing some particular piece of economic life, with all its complexities and interrelationships. That very night some political figure, in a five-minute telecast to the nation, will explain the whole thing simply and understandably in terms of heroes and villains. Consider the result if the Greeks of ancient times had been offered, in the Agora, a full and accurate scientific explanation of some natural phenomenon, a storm at sea, for example. There is the uneven heating from the sun, which brings about mass movements of air (believed by the Greeks to be caused by Aeolus); these movements are affected by the rotation of the globe (the Greeks thought the earth was flat) and by the changing seasons (which the Greeks explained by the story of Proserpina). "Nonsense!" some citizen would say to those few who had stayed to hear the matter out. "It is as we have long been told. The great god of the sea, Poseidon, is angry!"

In the myth of heroes and villains we have a poor explanation for economic events, an unfair basis for judging individuals, and method by which the public engages in self-delusion on a grand scale.

CHAPTER EIGHT

"After this, and, therefore, because of this"

That hen and egg are closely paired
Is certainly quite clear.
But which is cause and which effect
Doth not so quick appear.

There is a myth that explains economic events by means of whatever highly visible happening occurred immediately prior to or concurrent with the event in question. Thus we read on the financial pages that "stocks fell three points on news of the submission of the President's budget." Or the administrator points with pride to the fact that since his party has been in power the number of jobs has increased by four million. And a spokesman of the rival party views with alarm the fact that during this same period a million farms went out of existence.

There are limits to the effectiveness of this myth. Most people refused to believe that the Great Depression was caused by sun spots, though this was put forward as one of the explanations. It stretched credulity a bit too much. Nevertheless, the willingness to accept superficial explanations is quite strong.

The present myth is based on a fallacy known in logic as the "post hoc error." The label comes from a Latin phrase that describes this form of wrong reasoning: *post hoc, ergo propter hoc,* "After this, and, therefore, because of this." The Latin form is evidence that the error goes back a long way. The "post hoc error" or the "error of propinquity" is the form of reasoning that leads the rooster to think that his crowing causes the sun to rise, or Aesop's flea to exclaim, as he rides the chariot's axle, "What a dust do I raise!"

Did the stock market really respond to the President's budget, or was it the cumulative effect of unfavorable earnings? Did the Administration create the jobs and liquidate the farms, or was this the result of private decisions, stemming from impersonal economic forces? Did the sun spots cause the Depression, or did they just happen to come along at the same time? The answers suggest themselves. Highly publicized events were credited with causations that really lay with less dramatic and more complex economic forces. Very seldom will one be correct in attributing causation to whatever agent is most readily at hand.

When A and B are found to be related, this relationship may be of several kinds. It may be a spurious relationship, the result of chance, for example, as in the finding of F. L. Thomson that from 1929 to 1940 the height of women's hemlines was directly related to the height of the price level.

A and B may be related because both are dependent upon C. Thus, sales of lumber and cement tend to be positively related, not because one causes the other but because both are primarily dependent upon a third factor, the level of building activity. There will, of course, be other influential factors. Very rarely in the physical or economic world is a variable successfully explained by one force only.

If A and B are causally related, it is not automatically clear whether A caused B or B caused A. The Federal Reserve Bank may raise its official interest rate concurrently with rising commercial interest rates. But it would take more than superficial observation to determine whether the market was responding to the Board or the Board to the market.

Sometimes A and B are related in such fashion that they interact upon one another. Causation is mutual. For example, the hog cycle. High production of hogs causes a low price, and this in turn causes low production. The resultant low marketings bring on a high price, and this in time brings about high production, the cycle being completed in about four or five years. Who is to say whether price or production is the primary cause?

Everything that is a cause of something else is itself a result of foregoing causes. Except, of course, first causes, which are a concern of the theologian and the philosopher.

When it is possible to get hold of a reasoning person and engage his full attention for ten minutes, the "post hoc" myth can be demolished. But how many people are willing to listen, how many listeners are reasonable, and who will instruct them? And, if the lesson were learned, how long would it be retained?

That this myth is a bad one is almost self-evident to any thinking person. No great piece of writing; no major economic principle need be presented to make clear the error. At one stage, in fact, I struck the myth from my list. A man dedicated to the exorcising of myths wants worthy subject matter; the present one has no real merit except its stubborn capacity for survival.

As a matter of fact, this myth and those discussed in Chapters Six and Seven have all been inferior, and the last two progressively less meritorious than the first. Each has also required progressively less thought on the part of its adherent. To apply the myth that if the government does it, it is good (or bad), one need do no more than take a position regarding centralized decision-making. While this involves a considerable effort for some, for others it is not very demanding. To apply the myth of heroes and villains, one need only identify these characters, which is easier than to decide the philosophical question about government. To apply the myth that whatever comes after an event is a result of the event, one need only attribute causal importance to the most striking of a series of current or recent phenomena.

Nevertheless, this third myth of the low-grade category was retained because errors of considerable importance are attributable to it. One is the claim that the Republican Party is the party of depression because that party happened to be in office during the debacle of 1929–33. Another is the claim that the Democratic Party is the war party because that party happened to be in office during each of the past four wars. Triumphs are similarly treated; by the post hoc error, credit for a successful space program is attributed to the Administration that launched the rockets rather than the Administration that launched the program.

By the myth that whatever comes after the fact is the result of the fact, the President and the party in power are given credit or blame, far beyond their deserving, for the behavior of economic forces that are largely beyond their control. That they exercise some degree of control is acknowledged, and that there should be accountability is manifestly true. But the myth exaggerates both beyond reason.

The myth that what comes after the event is the result of the event is used to advantage by many people in public life. Political life is a cradle for myths, since the test of an allegation is its effectiveness rather than its veracity. For example, during World War II competitive markets for farm products were rising. Congressmen, seeing this, raised support prices, a highly visible act, and took credit for price increases. Public officials like to be associated with favorable news, knowing that some of the good feeling is likely to rub off on them. How beautiful, indeed, are the feet of those who bring glad tidings! And how bad the association with doleful events! We are told that in ancient times the king would reward those soothsayers who foresaw a favorable prospect and would execute those who foretold disaster.

By superficial reasoning, one who is associated with good or evil bears a causal relationship thereto and should be held accountable. To sort out the actual nature of the association and to allocate the appropriate amount of credit or blame is probably beyond the capacity and disposition of the public.

If one feels no real need for a logical or empirically justifiable set of economic ideas but is satisfied with something superficially plausible, the post hoc error is the one for him. It gives more answers per unit of effort than any other of the seven great myths we have studied. If one is a politician, operating with limited time and limited funds, intent above all on winning votes, this is the myth he needs. It will earn him more votes per unit of input than any other. If he is of the in-office party, all he need do is list everything good that has happened since his party was given responsibility and claim credit. If he is of the out-of-office party, he need only list the things that have gone amiss and blame them on his rival.

All of this may be offensive to people who value objectivity and fair treatment. How numerous such people are is an open question. It may be that the greatest myth of all is one to which I have not devoted a chapter — the myth that the public really wants the objective truth and will invest enough time and resources to get it. But I believe there is a real desire for understanding; that is the reason I have written this book.

We have now reviewed a number of myths, each of them a potential threat to the economy. The economy continues to perform well, despite the myths. How can this be?

For almost every myth, as we have seen, there is something like an opposite myth. The statesman, instinctively steering between them, often avoids them both. This is the great strength of a pluralistic system. The statesman seeks out that paradoxical, compromise-permitting middle ground so abhorred by the true believer. What is to the logician a conflict of testimony is to the statesman the manysidedness of truth. He picks his way, pragmatically, through a tangle of conflicting myths.

Many a politician continues to quote, in support of his position, myths he knows to be untrue. He would prefer not to do so. But to forego the use of weapons helpful to his cause would be akin to engaging in unilateral disarmament; there is no assurance that his rival would follow suit. If we were to jettison all the myths that pull us in one direction and leave intact all those that pull us in the other, our balanced strength would be lost. There are myths of "the right" and of "the left." Rather than to see only one variety destroyed, I concede that both should be allowed to survive. The preferred thing, of course, is the gradual erosion of both families of mythology through the process of economic education.

In any case, the economy has strength and resilience greater than most of us comprehend, great enough to survive much mythical belief.

On this reassuring note, let us leave the myths behind and turn to the accepted body of economic teaching. The ground is plowed. Now to sow the seed.

PART TWO

Doctrine

CHAPTER NINE

The competitive market

If an economic issue
You should try to understand,
You will surely find the answer
In supply and in demand.

Economics deals with less than the whole man. It concerns the activities of man in the satisfying of human wants. It assumes that self-interest is the governing motive in human affairs, that men are infallible in judging their interests and single-minded in pursuing them. This abstracted creature is called "economic man." Economics thus has something useful to say about the use of resources and the consumption of goods. But it explains very little above the love of a man for his family or his dedication to some deep cause or his appreciation of beauty.

Economics in its basic form is separate and apart from ideology. It is concerned with the use of scarce resources to attain given goals, and the economist is generally quite willing to let someone else state the goals. Thus, the Soviet Union needs the services of economists quite as much as the United States; economists in the two countries differ from one another chiefly in that they work toward different goals. Economics in its basic tenets is amoral, that is, lacking in ethical judgment. It applies as well to dope peddling as to food production.

Since economics deals with the use of scarce resources to

meet given goals, it is always concerned with the parceling out of restricted amounts of desired goods. Its focus is on human want. It was for this reason that Thomas Carlyle referred to economics as "the dismal science." And there is some merit in this appellation. With wants insatiable and means limited, the economist, who is concerned with the allocation process, is always saying "no" to somebody.

A man obtains goods or services from another in one of three ways: by theft, by gift, or by trade. Theft obviously involves a loss to the person from whom the article is obtained. Gifts involve some sacrifice on the part of the giver. Only with voluntary trade through the medium of the market is there an economic gain on the part of both parties. Thus, the immense usefulness of the market and the reliance placed on this institution by enlightened people. Let us examine the essential nature of the market, the key to modern economic activity.

The most effective way I have found for teaching the functioning of the market in a group setting is with an experiment involving the group itself. The following pages present actual results of such an experiment, conducted with two different sections of a college class in economics, section A numbering 31 students and section B, meeting the following hour, numbering 28.

DEMAND

On a warm fall afternoon here in Indiana I bring with me to the classroom a water glass full of cold sweet cider. I ask this question: "What is the *highest* price you would be willing to pay, now, for this glass of cider?" Each student writes his answer on a slip of paper. These are gathered, grouped for con-

110

venience into intervals having a range of 5 cents, and summarized as shown in Table VI.

TABLE VI

The highest price that would be paid	Number of students who would pay this price	Cumulative number of students who would pay this price
(cents)		
0–4	6	31
5–9	4	25
10–14	9	21
15–19	4	12
20–24	5	8
25–29	2	3
30–34	0	1
35–39	1	1
40–44	0	0
	31	

The replies, of course, measure the demand for cider in the class at this particular moment. Demand is desire, accompanied by means with which to acquire the desired object. Demand is measured by willingness to exchange money for the good in question. I ask each student for what is called his marginal demand price, that price at which he would buy, but a price so high that if it were to increase at all he would not buy. It is a price at which there is indifference as to whether one would buy or not; at the marginal demand price the money looks just about as good as the cider.

Obviously, the demand for cider varies tremendously from person to person. Six would pay no more than 5 cents; as a matter of fact, the individual reportings show that five of these would pay nothing at all. One would pay 35 cents rather than go without. Influencing this willingness to pay are such factors as the amount of money the student has, the degree of his thirst, and his liking for cider. Goods have different usefulness to different people, as noted in Chapter Three.

Now, clearly, the student who is willing to pay as much as 35 cents for a glass of cider would be happy to buy it for less. If the price were reduced to 25 cents he would buy gladly, and two additional people would buy, making three buyers in the market. If the price were further reduced, more students would enter the market until at a price of zero all 31 would take the cider.

GRAPH I

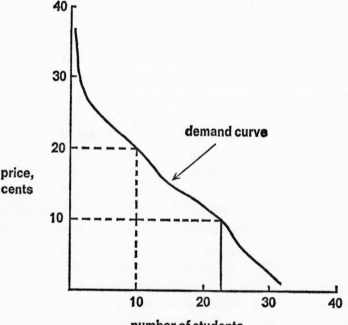

This economic interest can be shown in graphic fashion (Graph I) as a demand curve. (The curve is somewhat irregular because the students are few in number; with a larger group the curve would probably be smoother.)

This demand curve says that at a price of 20 cents about 10 glasses of cider would be demanded; if the price were cut in half, the quantity taken would be approximately doubled. The curve illustrates the law of demand, which states that, other things equal, the quantity of a good that will be purchased will increase as the price falls.

SUPPLY

After concluding this part of the experiment, section A leaves the room and section B comes in. Holding up the same glass I say: "Suppose each one of you had a glass of cider, like this, now. What is the *lowest* price that would induce you to part with it?" What I am asking each student for is what is called his marginal supply price, that price at which the holder of a good is willing to sell, but a price which, were it lower, would result in his retaining the article. At the marginal supply price, the supplier does not much care whether he sells or not. He gets about as much satisfaction from having the article as he does from receiving the money.

Each student writes his figure on a slip of paper. These are gathered and summarized as shown in Table VII. (As we accumulate these totals we move from the low to the high price, contrary to the procedure followed when we studied demand. This is necessary because, in our exercise, we approach the equilibrium quantity from one direction for demand and from the other direction with respect to supply.)

TABLE VII

The lowest price at which the student would sell his cider	Number of students who would sell at this price	Cumulative number of students who would sell at this price
(cents)		
0–4	0	0
5–9	2	2
10–14	11	13
15–19	3	16
20–24	4	20
25–29	7	27
30–34	0	27
35–39	0	27
40–44	1	28
	28	

Obviously, section B feels much the same as section A with respect to the utility of cider. The quoted prices have about the same average and cover about the same very wide range.

Now, plainly, at zero price no student could be induced to part with his cider. As the price increases, more students indicate they would offer. The price would have to get up to 40 cents before every one of the group would sell.

This situation can be graphed (Graph II) as a supply curve.

This curve says that at a price of 20 cents about 18 glasses would be offered. If the price should increase to 30 cents, 27 glasses would come on the market. The curve illustrates the law of supply, which states that, other things equal, the quantity of a good or service that will be offered on the market will increase as the price rises.

GRAPH II

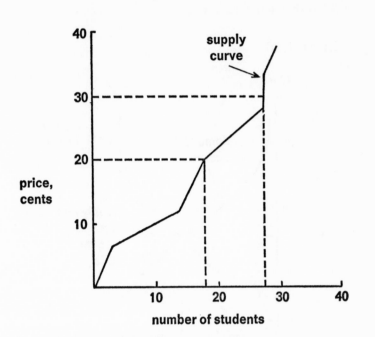

PRICE

What has been described up to now has actually occurred in my classroom. The next step follows, analytically. Suppose that we bring the two groups of students together in a large room. Each section B student has a glass of cider, each section A student is without. If they now behave as they said they would, trade will occur, the price of cider will be 16 cents and 15 glasses would change hands. This assumes that no one person would consume more than one glass. Although the assumption is not strictly correct, the essential principle here be-

115

ing set forth is valid. The resulting market activity can be graphed as shown in Graph III.

GRAPH III

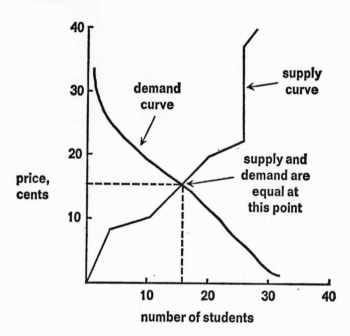

Why will 16 cents be the price? Because at any lower or higher price there would be unsatisfied demands or unaccepted offers. The volume of trade and the degree of total satisfaction would be less. For example, if in the early stages of discovering the appropriate price a tentative price of 10 cents were quoted, only eight glasses would be offered while 24 were demanded. Or suppose the opening price quotation were 20 cents. Then only 10 glasses would be desired, while 18 were offered. At a price of 16 cents and only at this price, supply and demand are equal, there is neither shortage nor surplus, the volume of

116

trade is at a maximum, and total satisfaction is likewise at a maximum. The urge to maximize voluntary trade is a reflection of the desire to increase the total of human satisfactions. There is no more important economic concept than the one set forth in this paragraph.

In my classroom "market," after some exploratory probing, only one price will prevail. If, temporarily, the price in one corner of the room is 18 cents and the price in the opposite corner is 12 cents, sellers will move to the high-priced sector and buyers to the low-priced. The price will soon be driven to the equilibrium level. This process, well established, is known as arbitrage; it illustrates what is called the "law of one price" which says that, after taking account of quality and locational differentials, only one price can prevail in a given market.

GAINS TO BUYERS AND SELLERS

Who gained in this laboratory experiment? Everyone who engaged in trade! The trading was completely voluntary, and only those who felt that they could better themselves in fact engaged in it. At least the expectation was for gain; there may have been some disappointments. Maybe some people discovered that they were not as thirsty as they had thought.

The biggest gainers were those eager buyers who would have been willing to pay a quarter or more but were able to buy for 16 cents, plus those eager sellers who would willingly have sold for a nickel but received three times as much. Those who gained least were the marginal buyers and sellers who were indifferent, or nearly so, with respect to trading. Those who did not engage in the trading neither gained nor lost.

The buyers who were able to purchase at a lower price

than their subjective valuation of the article received a net gain that economists call a "buyer's surplus." The sellers who received a higher price than the one at which they would have been willing to sell received a net gain called a "seller's surplus." The two gains are shown in Graph IV.

GRAPH IV

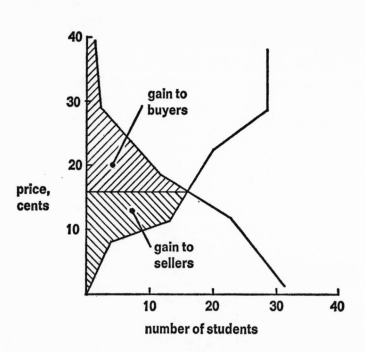

The total shaded area represents the total gains in utility, or in satisfaction, which resulted from trading.

No one who held the product in low esteem was forced to buy. No one who valued his cider highly was forced to part with it. If by being exploited we mean that a person is forced to surrender things of greater value than the things he receives,

118

then no one in this class exercise was exploited. There is immense wisdom in the old saying that "a fair exchange is no
robbery."

So much for the equilibrium situation, with the market
functioning freely.

PRICE SUPPORTS AND PRICE CEILINGS

Suppose that some regulatory agency should decide that,
in the interest of "protecting" cider sellers, price support

GRAPH V

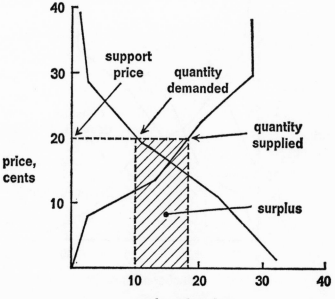

should be provided. Sixteen cents is thought to be too low a price; 20 cents becomes the official support level. But at this level only 10 glasses would be demanded while 18 are offered. A "surplus" of 8 glasses would appear, as shown in Graph V. There would now have to be some rationing of the right to sell, or else some program to dispose of the surplus.

Or suppose that the regulatory agency should decide that, in the interest of protecting the cider buyers, a price ceiling should be set. Ten cents might be considered a "fair" price to consumers. But at that price, 24 glasses would be demanded and only 8 would be offered. A "shortage" of 16 glasses would

GRAPH VI

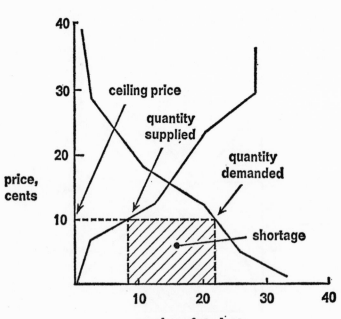

appear, as shown in Graph VI. It would now be necessary to subsidize production or ration consumption, or both.

The point is that if price is to be established by official act at some level other than the competitive level, strong administrative action will be necessary. An artificially maintained high price has as its inevitable companions regulated production or surplus disposal or both. An artificially maintained low price has as its companions rationed consumption or subsidized production or some combination thereof. If the market is not allowed to perform its functions, then regulatory action must undertake the allocations that the market itself would have made.

F. A. Pearson, Cornell economist, has said, "There is no economic problem which price will not solve." True enough, if we define the problem as a shortage or a surplus. We may not like the solution and may even deem it worse than the problem, but the forces of the market, if allowed to operate, will equate supply and demand at some level.

This simple classroom experiment has in it the very heart of economic principle. Most of economics is an elaboration or a qualification of the essentials here presented. One can study the effect of time, the number of buyers, differentiated markets, imperfect knowledge, regulatory activities, expectations, psychological factors, and changes in the medium of exchange. While all of these and many other considerations involve important modifications of our simplified model, none of them denies the model's essential truth.

Consider a few simple modifications. For example, suppose the temperature were to rise and thirsts therefore to increase. The students would then willingly pay a higher price; we would explain this by saying that demand increased. If this should happen and the supply were unchanged, the price would rise. Or supply might change for a variety of reasons. With changing demands and changing supplies, a very great number of different prices could occur, as is indeed the case in competitive markets.

CHAPTER TEN

Monopoly

To the market she went for to buy
And found all the prices too high.
With only one seller,
Misfortune befell her —
There was no other market to try.

In Chapter Nine we dealt with what economists call "perfect competition." In perfect competition there are many buyers and sellers; no one person can, by himself, exert any real influence on the quantity offered or the price obtained.

While perfect competition does not really exist in a strict sense, it is approached by many agricultural markets, such as those for fruits and vegetables. It is approximated in markets for industrial items produced by small firms, such as cottonseed oil and rough lumber. The market for maid service approaches the competitive model.

But for many markets perfect competition does not at all apply. It certainly does not apply for automobiles, steel, cigarettes, or unionized labor. For these commodities and services the behavior of a single firm or a single organization can have a marked effect on price.

Markets that do not meet the criteria of perfect competition are variously described:

Monopoly: (only one seller): A public utility may be the single supplier of power for a given area. A labor union may have complete control of the labor supply for some industry.

Oligopoly: (only a few sellers): Automobiles are produced by an oligopolistic industry.

Monopsony: (only one buyer): The Defense Department, buying military equipment, is of this type.

Oligopsony: (only a few buyers): The big chain stores, buying from farmers, are essentially oligopsonists.

In many cases the degree of control over price is less than may at first appear. A given railroad may be the only one to link two cities, but if its rates are too high the goods will move by truck. The United Steel Workers may have sole bargaining rights, industry-wide, but if wages get too high, the plants automate, or foreign steel comes in, or buyers turn to other metals and to concrete. If the Defense Department, as sole buyer, were to beat down the price below some given point, it would bankrupt the supplying firm and impair its source of needed material.

Some firms are large for the reason that such size carries with it genuine efficiency from the standpoint of production or marketing or both. Steelmaking firms have to be big, though not so big as some of them have become. Some firms strive to become larger, in part because of the dominant monopolistic position associated with size. They may go beyond the size that is most efficient from a production standpoint in order to gain the market power with which to set prices. This has been the case in some of the antitrust suits brought by the government. Or they may want size for some noneconomic reason, such as prestige.

The public tends to think of monopoly in terms of industry only, since it was industrial monopoly which first drew the nation's attention and led to the antitrust or anti-monopoly laws. This chapter will, therefore, treat monopoly in these familiar terms. But labor unions are also monopolistic if they exercise sole bargaining rights, and government farm programs are monopolistic if a legislated price is decreed and access to the market is restricted to those farmers whom government permits to sell. There is an element of truth to the statement that monopoly is prohibited in industry, condoned for labor, and required of farmers.

The basic forces that we call supply and demand for a particular good or service are similar, whether the industry is perfectly competitive or whether it is a monopoly. The demand curve is there, indicating restricted purchases as price increases. The supply curve is present; at a high price the supplying firm will be willing to provide more goods than will be the case if the price is low. The difference is that the monopolistic firm is in position to determine, for the industry, the supply of the commodity that will be offered, while the firm in perfect competition is unable to do so. This is a very great difference indeed.

Having this power, how will the monopolistic firm exercise it? The simple answer is that it will establish price and quantity so as to earn the greatest possible net revenue. But even here there are important qualifications. The monopolistic firm will have to take rival industries into account. Cotton must take account of rayon, metals must be aware of plastics. Furthermore, if the industry wishes to be in business over a period of years, as inevitably it does, it must be aware of its long-run as well as its short-run interest. Restricting output and pricing at a high level may increase current income but prevent the market-building required for long-run success. The concept used by the economist to describe the perfectly competitive market is often assailed as unreal, and indeed it is unrealistic in some respects. Knowledge is not perfect and adjustments are not instantaneous, though the idea of economic man considers them to be so. Likewise, the concept used to describe the monopolistic firm has its elements of unreality. The influence of rival industries, noneconomic motivations, and the inevitable question of long-run versus short-run considerations are seldom accounted for. Both perfect competition and monopolistic competition characterize extreme cases, cases that are approached but not realized.

The monopolistic industrial firm undertakes to learn the nature of the demand for its product. It tries to determine what quantities can be sold at a series of prices. It also studies its costs. Taking into account its long-run as well as its short-run interest, it will tend to increase output up to the point at which the cost of producing an additional item will equal the price at which that additional item will sell. Because of the nature of costs, this will ordinarily involve a profit on the items produced prior to the last one.

Once a firm has decided what price it will ask, the volume it can sell has been essentially predetermined. This is because of the nature of demand. Whether an industry is perfectly or imperfectly competitive, there is always some kind of demand curve. If a firm elects to name the price for its product, it can no longer exercise an independent decision as to volume. The idea that a firm can decide its price and then sell all it wants to at that price is one of the economic myths.

A firm engaged in perfect competition will accept demand in such form as it exists. Single-handed, it cannot influence demand, and if it did rival firms would share the gain. Hence firms in perfect competition will not advertise; a farmer does not advertise corn. On the other hand, a firm engaged in imperfect competition will do all in its power to influence demand. It will advertise, it will differentiate its products from those of rival firms, and it will differentiate its various products from one another. Thus it uses its capability to restrict volume, enhance price, and increase net income.

It is clear that, other things equal, restriction of volume undertaken to improve price and income will result in less efficient use of resources than would be the case with open competitive markets. The various trusts around the turn of the century had this effect. But it also is true that certain monopolistic companies have used their enhanced incomes for heavy outlays of research and thus have increased efficiency, lowered costs, and, ultimately, lowered prices. The American Telephone and Telegraph Company and DuPont are illustrations.

Firms in oligopolistic industries (only a few sellers) sometimes engage in collusion to fix prices or to limit output or to avoid "spoiling the market." A number of electrical equipment manufacturers were found guilty of this in a celebrated case some years ago; other firms in other industries have similarly conspired to restrain trade. Because of this collusion and because of the concentrated economic power possessed by monopolistic firms, American citizens generally react adversely to monopoly. Laws have been put on the books to prevent abuse of the public interest. The Federal Trade Commission, the Antitrust Division of the Department of Justice, and a number of other governmental agencies stand guard against monopolistic practices.

The public believes in some equivalence of economic power, some parity of position as regards the two sides at the bargaining table. One approach is the antitrust idea, through which we try to break up monopolistic concerns or restrict their power. The other approach has been called by J. K. Galbraith the theory of countervailing power, that is, the power of weak groups is built up to counter that of the dominant firms. The Wagner Act sought to give labor concentrated economic power, equivalent or superior to that of industry. Agricultural legislation has had as an objective the acquisition of concentrated economic power for farmers, with which they might meet, from an equal or superior position, the power of the great processing firms to whom they sell.

The objective of antitrust legislation and the objective of labor and farm legislation are similar in that both envision some equality of bargaining power on the part of the contending groups. The antitrust idea would pull down the strong to the level of the weak; farm and labor law would build up the weak to the level of the strong. Farmers would slug it out with industry in the legislative forum and in the market; labor would come to grips with industry in the Congress and at the bargaining table. Whether we should try to equate economic power at a high or at a low level is not a part of economic theory and hence not appropriate to this chapter. However, the reasoning that has led to these two approaches is based on economic thought.

Are monopoly and oligopoly on the increase in the United States? The popular view is that they are, yet the empirical evidence is not at all clear. A fair appraisal would seem to be that the degree of industrial concentration has not changed much in recent years.

Table VIII indicates that in 1947 the 50 largest companies accounted for 17 percent of all that manufacturers contributed to our total output. This percentage increased to 23 percent by 1954 and held at that level in 1958. The same essential picture emerges when we examine the experience of the 100 largest companies.

TABLE VIII

Percent of Value Added by Manufacture by the
Largest Manufacturing Companies in 1947, 1954, and 1958

Company size	Percent of value added by manufacture		
	1947	1954	1958
Largest 50 companies	17	23	23
Largest 100 companies	23	30	30

Source: Betty Bock and Jack Farkas, "Concentration in Manufacturing," Studies in Business Economics, No. 91, National Industrial Conference Board, New York, 1966, p. 18.

The degree and the trend of concentration vary markedly from one industry to another. Table IX shows a high and rising amount of concentration in the manufacture of motor vehicles and parts, with a relatively low and falling degree of concentration in meat-packing.

In recent years a new form of concentrated economic power has emerged through what are called "conglomerate mergers." R. J. Reynolds, commonly thought of as a seller of tobacco products, now also sells poultry, canned soups, catsup, and soft drinks. International Telephone and Telegraph has acquired an odd assortment of enterprises well described by their names: Hayes Furnace Company, Aetna Finance, Great International Life Insurance, Hamilton Management Company, Avis Rent-A-Car, ABC-Paramount (itself diversified, with broadcasting, theater, phonograph record, and publishing assets), and Airport Parking (with parking facilities at air terminals in 59 of the nation's largest cities).

129

TABLE IX

Percent of Industry Shipments by the
Largest Four Companies in Various Industries,
1947, 1954, and 1958

	Percent of industry shipments by the largest four companies			Number of companies in industry		
	1947	1954	1958	1947	1954	1958
Motor vehicles and parts	56	75	75	779	991	989
Petroleum refining	37	33	32	277	253	285
Motors and generators	59	50	47	224	266	317
Meat-packing products	41	39	34	1,999	2,228	2,646

Source: "Concentration Ratios in Manufacturing Industry: 1958," Bureau of the Census, U. S. Government Printing Office, Washington, D. C., 1962, Part I, Table 2, p. 10.

The main reasons for these mergers are the gains that come from maximizing the use of high managerial skills over a wide area, plus the ability of a strong central company to carry a weak subordinate through a period of low earnings associated with market development or reorganization.

The public has not yet made up its mind about conglomerate mergers, and the law is largely silent about them. Undoubtedly some expression of the public interest will be forthcoming in the years ahead.

One thing remains abundantly clear, based on empirical evidence. Despite such monopolistic practices as occur, despite such restraint of trade as prevails, despite such conspiracy against the consumer as may elude the regulatory agencies, the American level of living continues to rise. Whether living levels would rise faster or slower in the absence of monopolistic power, or how the relative income positions of different economic groups would be altered if perfect competition prevailed—these things cannot be established with any degree of certainty. The citizen's misgivings regarding monopoly perhaps emanate more from his basic dislike for concentrated or unbalanced economic power than from demonstrable injury to his level of living. If this is true, the crucial judgments regarding imperfect competition are to be given by all the social sciences acting together rather than by the economist alone.

CHAPTER ELEVEN

Economics
and the consumer

If our hearts you'd weigh,
Beware of our pretending.
Forget the things we say,
And scrutinize our spending.

Why does the consumer spend his money the way he does? Why do some people buy items of solid usefulness while others buy gewgaws? Why does one neighbor save a large sum while another goes deeply in debt? Why do some people respond to fads while others do not? Why does advertising seem to be effective with certain people and some commodities but not with all? Why does one man buy items to meet what appear to be his genuine needs while another buys to keep up with the Joneses? Why do some people work hard so as to be able to purchase many items and other people loll around, seemingly content with much leisure and few purchases? Without some understanding of economics, particularly consumption economics, our individual behavior appears chaotic.

The questions just posed were answered in part in Chapter Three, wherein utility was defined as the ability of a good or a service to satisfy a want. There we made a great point of the fact that wants and desires are unique to the individual. We have said repeatedly that economics is without ethical judgment as to the merits of various wants. Thus, if a man desires a

133

new car not just for transportation, but to impress his neighbors (conspicuous consumption, Thorstein Veblen would have called it), this is a sufficient motive from an economic standpoint. If a man has such an avid thirst for current goods that he borrows heavily and puts himself at the mercy of his creditors, economics can readily accommodate this behavior within its principles. Conversely, a man may experience gratification from denying himself the current consumption of goods so as to have more goods later, or he may experience some deep gratification from saving — he may even wish to save so as to be the wealthiest man in the cemetery. While such deportment may make very little sense to an observer, the important fact is that it expresses the value preferences of the individual in question.

We cannot effectively treat these concepts with the very limited set of tools thus far made available. We need several additional ideas, not easy to comprehend, the presentation of which has perhaps been too long delayed. One of these is marginality, a key idea introduced by the so-called Austrian school of economists a hundred years ago. The idea, as it applies in consumption economics, is that a man's buying behavior is determined not by the average satisfaction he obtains from having consumed a stock of goods but from his satisfaction in buying an additional or an incremental or a marginal item. (We dealt briefly with this matter in Chapter Nine when we considered the marginal demand for cider.) Thus a man might have a great liking for his cuff links, might get great utility from them, might enjoy a considerable "consumer surplus" from having purchased them, but the satisfaction he might obtain from another pair of cuff links of precisely the same kind might be very low indeed. He is receiving great utility from his cuff links but this will not lead him to purchase another pair, that is, an incremental or a marginal set. And the economist is interested in gladness of heart only as it has some market impact.

This takes us close to a problem that has puzzled people for centuries, and also gives us an answer to it. What is the distinction between "value in use" and "value in exchange"? This is the question that troubled Adam Smith. He asked, in his *Wealth of Nations,* "How is it that water, which is so very useful that life is impossible without it, has such a low price — while diamonds, which are quite unnecessary, have such a high price?" The answer comes out clearly if we understand consumption economics. The price of water in a competitive market is determined not by the usefulness of those quantities already consumed, but by the utility of the marginal amount, the additional gallon. With water so abundant, our remaining unmet needs are few and we will not pay much for that marginal amount. Diamond jewelry, on the other hand, has the ability to satisfy wants, whether these are related to the use of diamonds for engagement rings, to the giving of prestigious gifts, to express our esteem to someone dear, or to impress our friends. Diamonds are few indeed. Relatively few of our felt needs for diamonds have been met; the marginal utility and hence the price of diamonds is therefore high. Such pricing and such behavior might seem nonsensical to a person devoid of aesthetic sense, without regard for tradition, with concern for only the bare necessities of human existence, or without economic understanding. But to a person aware of the richness and complexity of human experience and with some appreciation for economic principle, consumer behavior is quite understandable.

We have been drawing here on a key principle — the principle of diminishing utility. This holds that the satisfaction gained from the use of the second of a series of items is less than the satisfaction obtained from the first, and so on. How much would one pay for a second meal immediately after consuming the first? Obviously much less, and this despite the fact that the meal was identical and cost as much to prepare.

The principle of diminishing utility tells us why a large supply of a given good, other things equal, will sell only at a lower price. It takes a decline in price to persuade the consumers to buy additional items. The amount of change in consumption that can be induced by a given change in price is an economic measurement of major importance, known through economic studies. Table X gives some representative items.

TABLE X

	Percent change in quantity purchased related to a 10 percent decline in retail price
Lamb	17.8
Beef	6.8
Milk	1.4
Potatoes	1.1

Source: G. E. Brandow, "Interrelationships Among Demands for Farm Products and Implications for Control of Market Supply," Pennsylvania Agricultural Experiment Station Bulletin 680, 1961, p. 59.

We now come to another key idea in consumption economics, the principle that people will adjust their purchases so that marginal utilities per dollar will be equal for every good or service. What does this mean? Simply this: that a consumer, if he is free, will spend his money where he expects to get the most satisfaction. Here we encounter economic man again. He will keep buying more of the thing that gives him the greatest satisfaction until, through diminishing utility, the good in question yields the same amount of satisfaction per dollar as do other items. He may be disappointed in his purchase, as Ben Franklin was when he found that he had paid too much for his whistle. Other things equal, however, a man will not spend his money for a given good if some other good, also available for purchase, would give him greater satisfaction. Thus a man's actual purchases will tell us more about his value judgments than could be learned in any other way. Many modifications of this principle are needed, of course. Cigarettes come at 30 cents per pack, a shoeshine at 25 cents, an automobile at $3,000. The man's marginal utilities can more nearly be equated for cigarettes and shoeshines than for cigarettes and cars. Some items are too "lumpy" to fit neatly into the concept.

For those who like the precision and rigor of mathematical expression, the fundamental condition of consumer equilibrium can be written as follows:

$$\frac{\text{Marginal utility of Good 1}}{\text{Price of Good 1}} = \frac{\text{Marginal utility of Good 2}}{\text{Price of Good 2}} = \frac{\text{Marginal utility of Good 3}}{\text{Price of Good 3}} =$$

$$\frac{\text{Marginal utility of Savings Bond}}{\text{Price of Savings Bond}} = \frac{\text{Marginal utility of leisure time}}{\text{Income foregone in order to enjoy leisure}} = \text{Common marginal utility}$$

Now, certainly no person will calculate this out accurately. One could not very well punch all these values on IBM cards, run the deck through the machine, and come out with a decision as to whether he should buy lawn furniture or go to the movies. Luckily no one is so deadly earnest about the matter. But even if the values are in large part subjective and unique to the individual, the principle is certainly valid.

However, if we could quantify this system accurately for

a particular person at a given moment, we still would not have very much useful information. For the quantities are dynamic. Obviously, changes in prices of individual goods or services will change the manner in which we adjust to the equation. An increase in the price of beef will result in a diminution in the consumption of beef and an increase in the consumption of pork. An increase in one's income will alter the quantities; the outlay for entertainment will probably increase and expenditures for potatoes will fall. As one grows older the marginal utility obtained from a sports car will probably decline while that to be had from digestive remedies will probably increase. Advertisements change the pattern. Fads change it. Fluctuations in business affect anticipations and hence modify the equation.

One reason this system will probably never be computerized is that each consumer has his own built-in computer, a marvelous, delicate piece of calculating equipment, able subjectively to anticipate with some degree of accuracy the utilities to be gained from the purchase of many thousands of items, capable of reckoning these against their respective costs, quickly comparing these with one another, and judging each and all against his ability to buy. The human mind, thus at work, can rapidly accept changes in coefficients. It can drop or add variables and come out with a decisive answer in a split second. This is what is happening when the housewife, shopping in the supermarket, hesitates a moment before she selects her Sunday roast.

Skill of this kind does not spring magically into being. The child does not have it. The tribesman, living in a subsistence economy, does not have it. Some people develop it to a marked degree; they are to be found at all levels of economic life. Among the poor this skill is a great asset for the wise use of limited resources. Skill in equating marginal utilities may be acquired by study or by experience. The better forms of advertising contribute to a buildup of this skill. The constant exercise of decision-making in buying goods and services and in keeping the household budget is perhaps the best discipline.

Those people who trouble to study the quality, utility, and price of consumption goods perform a valuable public service. By insisting, insofar as they are able, before they buy a good, that it have genuine promise of satisfying wants, they exercise a discipline that "keeps the market honest." They discover shoddy merchandise, and warn their friends about it. They compare prices and report them. As a result of this close scrutiny, firms that sell inferior goods or overcharge their customers are made to change their ways or are forced out of business. Many a person who does not consider his purchases carefully is able to skip this chore because other consumers have been astute buyers and have eliminated the inefficient or predatory sellers. It reflects no discredit on regulatory agencies to say that the consumer himself is one of the most potent forces in keeping markets economically efficient and socially useful.

Consumption theory makes understandable things which would otherwise be confusing; it points out how limited income may yield the most satisfaction; it shows how the consumer polices the market system; and it renders obsolete a number of economic myths. One who fully understands consumption economics will have deep reservations about price-fixing and rationing. He will be aware of the inequity of equal rewards and he will have high regard for voluntary exchange.

CHAPTER TWELVE

The economics of production

Labor, Land, and Capital,
Efficiently combined
By Management, through Enterprise,
Is what you here will find.

We deal here with the way the individual firm attempts to maximize the output it can obtain with any given cost outlay. In simpler terms, the objective in production economics is to use managerial skill in putting together land, labor, and capital so as to earn the largest possible net returns. Production economics is therefore the make-or-break discipline for every factory, farm, and other place of business. The principles are general and useful in understanding the production of any good or service.

Economists speak of land, labor, and capital as the factors of production. Sometimes management is included in the list, sometimes it is considered as a special factor, exercising control over the others.

Goods and services are produced by combining these factors of production. The decision-maker in the steel mill exercises judgment (management) in acquiring raw materials (obtained from land) and in employing steel workers (labor) in his plant (capital) to make steel. The shoeshine boy may combine all of the factors of production in his own person. He is an enterpriser (manager); he may have a space six-feet square (land), possess a chair and a brush (capital), and do his own work (labor). A farmer, a dry-goods merchant, and a gas station operator likewise put together the factors of production to turn out their special goods and services. In each case the purpose of production is assumed to be the earning of profit, the maximizing of net returns.

Each of the factors of production has its reward, bearing a different name. The return to land is called rent. The return to labor is wages, the return to capital is interest, the return to management is profit or loss, as the case may be.

The manager is assumed to be interested in the highest return. He ordinarily cares relatively little whether this return comes from one or another combination of these individual factors.

The number of possible combinations of the factors of production is large. Suppose, for example, that for a particular firm there are four possible levels of input for each of the four factors. There could then be 256 distinct combinations! In order to make the problem manageable, the economist ordinarily examines the relationship between individual factors and production one at a time. This is called the input-output relationship, or the production function. The manager looks at this input-output relationship not in terms of a single average figure but in marginal terms. In Chapter Eleven, while considering consumption, we studied *marginal utility*. Now, while considering production, we study *marginal physical product*. The marginal physical product is the increase in output that results from a given increase in input of one of the factors, with the others held constant. One of the best illustrations of the input-output

142

relationship is to be found in the application of fertilizer to cropland. Table XI shows the results of a potato experiment in Maine.

TABLE XI

Inputs of 4–8–7 Fertilizer and Output of Potatoes

Fertilizer input (500-pound units)	Total yield attributable to fertilizer (bushels per acre)	Additional or marginal output for each added 500-pound unit of fertilizer (bushels per acre)
0	0	
		103
1	103	
		71
2	174	
		49
3	223	
		34
4	257	
		24
5	281	
		17
6	298	
		10
7	308	

Source: Earl O. Heady, *Economics of Agricultural Production and Resource Use,* Prentice-Hall, New York, 1952, p. 36.

It will be noted that as more fertilizer is applied, total production first increases rapidly, then begins to level off. This illustrates one of the most important of economic laws, the law of diminishing returns. Stated formally:

If the input of one resource is increased by equal increments per unit of time while the inputs of other resources are held constant, total product output will increase, but beyond some point the resulting output increases will become smaller and smaller.

If input increases are carried far enough, total output will reach a maximum and thereafter will decrease. In the potato experiment, too much fertilizer makes the soil toxic and reduces output. Too much labor on a given job will find the workmen getting in one another's way, thus reducing production.

The task, therefore, is to discover the most profitable level of input, recognizing that the law of diminishing returns will be at work. This will depend on the price of the input and the price of the product as well as on the physical input-output ratio. The principle is that, beginning from a low level, more and more inputs will be supplied until the cost of the added input equals the value of the resulting product. In economic shorthand, this is the point at which marginal cost equals marginal revenue. To stop short of this level is to forego income. To go beyond it is to reduce returns.

Thus the theory — neat, tidy, and logically unassailable. In the chart or in the equation, it looks precise and convincing. But there are problems! Some producers have no intention of maximizing income, perhaps preferring a less competitive, less strenuous life. Furthermore, very few firms can know their marginal cost curves with accuracy. They may be able to account rather well for their costs at the level of input that did indeed occur, but they have difficulty in knowing what their costs and returns would have been at other levels. Furthermore, other inputs do not stay constant, so as to permit easy appraisal of the input-output relationships for one factor. As a matter of fact, the most profitable experiences are often obtained when the inputs of several factors are changed at the same time. For example, in our potato experiment, the effect of fertilizer on crop yields would depend on the variety of seed planted, on the availability of water, and on tillage practices. The effect of using more capital in a factory will depend on whether the labor input is changed or held stable. It is not given to man to be able to know all of these intricate relationships at once, though management steadily becomes more sophisticated and better able to estimate them.

The typical manager learns what he can from his own experience and from accounting. He tries to learn what he can from other firms in circumstances like his own. He develops some intuitive judgments, based on his experience. He introduces some degree of venturesomeness into the operation. He holds in his mind some concept of the relationships which govern the performance of his firm, probably a concept which conforms fairly well to the theory of production economics, which in all likelihood he has never studied. Thus equipped, he exercises his best judgment as to how resources should be combined. Circumstances differ; how else explain a farm of 160 acres adjoining one of 1,000 acres, with physical resources apparently similar? How explain the supermarket and the corner grocery, with vastly different organizational forms, yet apparently competing effectively with one another? These variations do not deny the validity of the theory; it is quite possible that differences in only one factor, managerial skill, can account for many of the observed variations.

The fact that most managers have never heard about marginal cost and marginal revenue does not impair the theory. Practice preceded the theory in any case. The theorist has merely described in logical fashion what the good practitioner was already doing. But in formalizing the theory he provides a useful frame of reference and sets up a concept that permits the alert manager to improve his combination of resources and boost his profits.

Suppose a manager has done a good job, and has somehow managed to put together the factors of production so as to maximize his profits. Can he congratulate himself, stabilize his operation, and continue to earn large profits? By no means. If some new technique comes along, the input-output relationships are changed and he must adjust his operation. If the cost of one factor increases relative to another — labor costs, let us say, rise relative to capital costs — he must reduce his use of labor and increase his capital investment. If the price of his product changes, the whole structure may need to be recast.

So far we have been thinking of production as if it consisted of a single item. Actually there may be many products. Cattle, wheat, and feed grain for the farmer. Sales of gasoline and the servicing of cars for the filling station. A full line of goods for the hardware merchant. Trucks, cars, busses, and military equipment for General Motors.

How choose the most profitable volume for these various articles? They may be joint products, produced in association with one another (as lead and zinc in mining). They may compete directly with one another for resources (a professor teaching a course in economics and another course in accounting). They may be complementary products in that the production of one increases the production of another (as in a good crop rotation). For each of these products there are input-output relationships or production functions of a physical nature that may or may not be known. To determine the most profitable level of output for half a dozen different products, some joint, some competitive, some complementary, turned out by combining four different factors of production, and all

146

of this in a setting of changing technology and shifting prices for factors and products — this is the problem of management. What a problem! Overwhelming for the timid, challenging for the venturesome.

To the firm producing several products, the general objective remains the same, to maximize net returns, to get the most income from a given quantity of resources. It is not necessary in order to achieve this objective that the marginal revenue from each item be equal to its marginal cost. Some companies produce certain items at a loss in order to have a "full line"; more net income is added by the enhanced position of the major product than is lost on the one that fails to cover its own cost.

The possibility of producing several products brings us to another basic economic concept, the idea of "opportunity cost." There are several ways of figuring costs. One is the customary accounting method. Another is to consider the "cost" of producing one article to be the sacrifice of the opportunity to produce a second. The cost of producing corn may be the returns that would have been obtained by producing the next best alternative, perhaps soybeans. This simple idea helps explain much about human behavior. For example, think of the handicraft worker in the Appalachian Highlands engaged in wood carving for the tourist trade. At most estimates of wage rates, his cost of production is fantastically high and one can hardly see how he would keep going. But his next best opportunity may be very poor; in this respect his opportunity cost is very low indeed and he stays in business.

Several other key economic ideas need mention. One of these is the principle of comparative advantage. We have earlier seen that in voluntary specialization and exchange, which is the powerful source of economic advancement, both parties gain. The principle of comparative advantage describes which commodities will be produced and exchanged, and which way trade will move.

My illustration has deliberately been kept simple. Indiana has an absolute advantage over Oklahoma in production per acre of both corn and wheat:

Bushels per acre, 1965

	Indiana	*Oklahoma*
Corn	94	34
Wheat	34	28

In Indiana corn outyields wheat by 2.8 to 1. In Oklahoma corn outyields wheat by a lesser ratio, 1.2 to 1. Corn does better, relative to wheat, in Indiana than in Oklahoma. In Indiana corn has both an absolute and a comparative advantage. Indiana specializes in corn. In Oklahoma wheat yields .85 as much as corn. In Indiana wheat yields only .37 as much as corn. Thus wheat does better, relative to corn, in Oklahoma than in Indiana. So Oklahoma specializes in wheat. She may not have an absolute advantage in wheat but she has a comparative advantage. It is this principle that has me working at my desk and hiring my home painted, even though I might be able to paint more square feet per hour than the man I hire. I have an absolute advantage over him in both teaching and painting. But I have a comparative advantage in teaching and he in painting, so we specialize and sell our services. It is this principle which underlies international trade, regional specialization, individual choice of vocation, and the enterprises selected for a given firm. It is this principle which keeps constructively employed not only our best resources but the others as well.

The law of supply, introduced earlier, has great importance in production economics. The law has it that if price of a product rises, other things equal, production will increase. Why is this so? Primarily it is because of another law also discussed earlier, the law of diminishing returns. As noted, a firm presumably tries to make the most money possible. Maximum returns occur when marginal revenue equals marginal cost. In keeping with the principle of diminishing returns, marginal costs ordinarily rise as the size of the firm increases. At the point of maximum profit, marginal costs, equal to marginal revenue, will in fact be rising. If the price of the product goes up, marginal revenue rises and the firm can find it profitable to employ more resources, to push farther along the curve of diminishing returns, profitably incurring the greater costs involved in this expanded effort. It will make marginal returns equal to marginal costs at a new and larger volume of production than before. It is by this mechanism that consumers, bidding up the price, can induce producers to supply more goods.

One major idea remains for consideration in this skeleton outline of production economics: the relationship between the price of the product and cost of production. Here we must distinguish between the short run and the long run, the short run being a time too brief to permit adjustment in the use of resources and the long run being of such duration that resources may be reallocated.

In the short run, according to the English economist Alfred Marshall, the relationship of price to cost may be not at all close. The price of a morning's catch of fish, sold on the pier, may be far higher or lower than the cost of bringing them in, depending primarily on the size of the catch. But in the long run the price of fish — or beef or anything else — will be fairly close to the cost of producing it, including the necessary reward for management as part of the cost. If the price is above cost for a time, additional resources will be brought into production and the price will be brought down. If price is below cost, some firms will be forced out of business, production will decline, and price will rise.

We have been focusing primarily on competitive enterprises, that buy their production items in a free market and sell in open competition with other firms. If the market is monopolistic, then management will operate as indicated in Chapter Ten.

Production is principled, not whimsical. Millions of managers put together the factors of production on America's farms and in her businesses, experimenting, innovating, and venturing. They respond to the signals given to them by the consumers. The result is a supply of goods and services that for variety and quality exceed those available to any other people on the globe. Such a marvel cannot occur by chance, ungoverned or undisciplined. To know how it happens is one of the rewards for studying economics.

But how close do our American business firms come to maximum efficiency, to combining the factors of production in truly optimum fashion, to managing their firms in accordance with economic theory? Other things equal, probably closer in a fairly stable industry than in one that is rapidly changing and probably closer if management is experienced than if untrained. Evidence indicates that business comes closer to optimum efficiency in an industry that is competitive, with the judgment of many individuals brought to bear, than in an industry that is heavily regulated, with management restrained from full use of its capacity for decision-making. But it seems likely that even under the best of circumstances we fall far short of true maximization in the use of productive resources. If the baseball player truly optimized all of his motions, he would hit a home run every time; if the business manager's judgment were always perfect, economic life would be more productive, though perhaps duller. The fact that the batter and the manager hit the home run only rarely is what makes the game interesting.

CHAPTER THIRTEEN

Rewards

We can tell you what is costly
And prevent your going bust.
We can tell you what's efficient,
But can't tell you what's just.

We have now seen how land, labor, capital, and management are used to produce a country's goods and services. The next question is: How are these factors of production rewarded for their contribution? Jointly they create the gross national product. How are the rewards that come from the joint product distributed among the landowners, the workers, the financial community, and the managers who brought these rewards into being?

The question relates to what the economist calls distribution theory. There is probably more intellectual wreckage strewn in this arena than in any other within the confines of our subject. The now discarded wages fund theory, the iron law of wages, and the Marxist labor theory of value, all of which we found to be erroneous, originated in this sector of economics.

Present economic teaching treats prices of the factors of production (land, labor, capital, and management) just as it treats prices of the goods and services produced by these agents. The principles of price determination as discussed in

Chapters Nine and Ten have general validity. In a competitive market, supply and demand determine the rent of land, the wages of labor, the interest on capital, and the reward to enterprise as well as the price of beef, scrap iron, and haircuts. If the setting is monopolistic, the analytical concept must be that of an imperfectly competitive market, whether one deals with products or with the factors of production.

The demand for the factors of production comes from the usefulness of the products supplied therefrom. Land, labor, capital, and management do not themselves gratify wants; the demand for them is a derived demand. But it is a real demand nonetheless and it is responsive to the same analytical tools.

Does this analysis mean that land, labor, capital, and management are rewarded in proportion to their true contribution? We cannot say. For output is the joint product of all four. If any one of the factors of production were lacking, output would be zero. The worker is right in saying that without his labor there would be no production, and the employer is equally right in saying that without his enterprise there would be no jobs. But these are not valid arguments for claiming the whole reward of the joint effort. That we are an interdependent society no longer needs to be demonstrated to intelligent people. There is no practical way by which one can accurately attribute to the separate contributors credit for the thing they have jointly produced.

But if we cannot establish that market-determined rewards to land, labor, capital, and management are in accordance with their true contribution, neither can we establish that one factor is being compensated disproportionately. Even if such determination could be made, it would still not be possible for

154

the economist to say that a given reward was fair or unfair. This we studied in Chapter Three. The problem of equity is not primarily in the economist's jurisdiction.

Rewards to the factors of production are arrived at in accordance with the principles of price determination. As we saw in Chapter Nine, price in the competitive market is established at a level at which certain buyers and certain sellers are marginal, that is, indifferent as to whether they engage in exchange or not. When price is "discovered" at this point, the price applies to all buyers and sellers in the market (the law of one price). Thus if marginal sellers of hogs are just barely willing to supply their product at 20 cents per pound, other sellers can obtain no more than that. If marginal buyers are just barely willing to pay 20 cents, all buyers have to pay that much.

This brings us to an important principle, namely, that in a competitive market the reward to a factor of production will tend to equal that level at which the marginal supplier is willing to offer it. Thus the return to a particular type of labor in a competitive market will tend to equal the level at which the marginal laborer is willing to work. The return to capital will tend to equal the interest rate at which the marginal financier is willing to lend his money.

Suppose this reward is lower than society, acting through its representatives in Congress, deems appropriate. What obstacles are encountered in raising it? One of the chief obstacles turns out to be those who supply the factor in question! If a minimum wage law is to be effective, there must be some way of overcoming the behavior of those willing to work for less. If parity of income is to be provided for farmers, there must be some way of preventing farmers from offering their services

155

for a lower return. If one is to increase the returns to a factor of production, he must somehow thwart the economic inclinations of those involved.

Land, which was once thought to be distinct from the other factors of production, is really no different; its price is determined by the supply of it relative to the demand for it. There is this uniqueness about it, that its supply cannot be easily increased. Drainage, irrigation, and land-leveling can somewhat increase the total quantity, but only to a limited extent.

As noted in Chapter Ten, if land or labor or capital is controlled by a monopoly, then the return thereto will be determined by the principles of monopolistic competition. Farmland in the United States is bought and sold in what is essentially a competitive market, whereas the pricing of land in a feudalistic society, to the extent that it is sold at all, tends to be monopolistic. Wages of farm labor are competitive; wages of unionized labor are best analyzed by use of the monopolistic model. American capital markets are generally competitive, while in many less-developed countries credit is extended by moneylenders who operate locally on a semimonopolistic basis. To understand how the social dividend is shared, one first determines which concept to use and then proceeds with his analysis.

The economist's common tendency is to analyze returns within a fairly rigorous set of assumptions, considering "everything else equal" or unchanged. We examine returns to farmers or laborers or professional people as if none of them had any alternatives. This greatly simplifies the analysis, though it invalidates the findings. We tend to treat the economy as if it were a plastic ice-cube tray, in which the sections retain the water that is poured into them. Actually, the economy is much more like a tray with a loose, removable divider, so that water seeps through the cracks and finds it level, irrespective of where it is first poured. In an assumed world of "everything else equal" a firm or an industry can capture such gains as result from increases in efficiency. And the firm will bear, by itself, the full consequences of any adverse event. In the real world the assumption of "other things equal" does not hold. Gains from efficiency are widely distributed and adversity is shared. This takes time, of course. Much time! More time than most people are willing to grant.

The following generalized table shows the situation during the past generation for various workers, organized and unorganized, who either have or have not achieved efficiency gains.

Worker	Status	Increase in efficiency	Behavior of real wages
Farm worker	unorganized	very great	rose gradually
Manual laborer	unorganized	zero	rose gradually
Barber	unionized	zero	rose gradually
Automobile worker	unionized	very great	rose gradually

The efficiency gains achieved by the first and fourth groups appear superficially in the form of increased output per man-hour. Actually, they are achieved largely through equipping the worker with better tools. Thus they reflect, in part, a contribution of capital. While great efficiencies were achieved by farmers and workers in the automobile industry, these workers were not able to capture all these gains for themselves. They were shared with barbers, who have made no appreciable efficiency gains during the past generation, and with unskilled manual laborers, who probably dig no more dirt in a day than did their fathers.

How can gains be won by those who have done nothing to earn them? Because, over time, workers are mobile. During years past, people left agriculture and unskilled manual labor in great numbers for higher-paying jobs. Thus they managed to equate, in a rough way, the supplies of and demands for labor in these various vocational fields at something like their long-established normal relationships. The efficiency gains achieved in certain sectors of the economy were dispersed throughout. The impact of adversity was softened by an economy that was humanitarian in effect if not intent. The fact that some people made the adjustment lessened the need for others to adjust. The restrictionist practices of unionized automobile workers and barbers made possible some favorable differential above that of their unorganized brethren. But this differential evidently had some tolerable limit.

Inequality of rewards, to the degree that it exists, disappoints the man who holds in his mind an ideal of equality. On the other hand, the obvious diffusion of well-being confounds the analyst who thinks in terms of "everything else equal," distresses the man who hopes to hold for himself the total gains made through increased efficiency, and, through the sharing of burdens warms the heart of the humanitarian.

There is less of a differential in rewards than in contributions. The competitive society ingeniously — and, in my judgment, appropriately — thwarts those who would hold their gains closely to themselves and alleviates the problems of those in stagnant or declining industries. In the long run we advance more as members of a total society than as individual persons or as vocational groups.

158

CHAPTER FOURTEEN

Money, credit, and prices

Filthy lucre, root of evil,
Fitting food for moth and weevil,
Corrupter of a million men,
The foulest thing that's ever been!
I like it!

Kin Hubbard said that only one fellow in ten thousand under-stands the currency question, and we meet him every day. The ratio of myth to reality is a high one in the field of money and prices. Our task in this chapter is to sort out the major ideas concerning money that are both true and relevant, and to present these as clearly as possible. This chapter is probably the most difficult one in the book.

The professional literature on money, credit, banking, and prices is generally good and reasonably well agreed upon. The difficulty comes from trying to graft this good bud onto a faulty rootstock.

The importance of money may be judged from the fact that it constitutes half of every business transaction. A sale involves the exchange of some article for a sum of money. The price, therefore, reflects the influence of both the article and the money. If the price of shoes changes over a period of time, the change may be a result of something that happened to shoes, to money, or to both. These changes may be relatively mild, as in the United States, where the consumer price index rose at a

159

little more than one percent per year for the decade ending in 1965. They may be rapid, as in Brazil, where prices have risen at an average rate of about 50 percent per year during the past seven years. Or there may be runaway inflation, as in Germany in December of 1923 when prices zoomed to an index of 142 trillion, with the level of 1910–14 equal to 100. Prices may move down as well as up. From 1920 to 1921 prices of basic commodities in the United States fell 46 percent. From 1929 to 1933 prices of these same commodities fell 47 percent.

Most big changes in prices originate on the money side of the exchange process. The explanation for a surge of inflation or the downward spiral of deflation is more likely to be found in something that happened to the single item in which prices of all goods and services are denominated, money, than in something that happened to the hundreds of thousands of separate items for which money is exchanged.

If, when the price level changes, prices of all goods and services would change at the same time and by the same amount, there would be no problem, since no price is high or low except by comparison. But when the average of all prices moves up or down, some prices change sharply and some remain unchanged. With inflation or deflation the face value of a thirty-year mortgage or a long-term bond or a life insurance policy changes not at all. The administratively determined salary of a school teacher changes very slowly. Retail prices, which represent a mixture of volatile and slowly changing costs, change moderately. Fastest changing of all are wholesale prices of raw materials. Thus a major price change distorts the buying and selling situation of almost every individual. The debtor gains by inflation and loses by deflation. The widow depending on an annuity has an exact opposite experience. People blame one another for injustices that have their origin not in acts of exploitation or ill will but in the fluctuating value of the currency.

The dollar is the medium in which all contracts are denominated. It is the measure of value. If the dollar itself is changing in value, how are we to build a satisfactory economy? It is like trying to build a house with a rubber yardstick. The more advanced we become, the more long-term contracts we write, the more important it is that the dollar be relatively stable in value. Thus one of our major concerns with money is that it be so managed as to produce a reasonably stable level of prices.

Another major concern with money comes from its effect on the level of business activity. Money is a lubricant for the economic machine. When money is relatively abundant and prices are rising, enterprise is encouraged. The man who increases his inventory or puts up a building finds his net worth rising. The man who borrows money to launch a venture finds that he can retire his debt with relative ease. With deflation, the whole process is reversed. The man who does best is the hoarder, who keeps his money in the bedticking; it will buy more as the price level falls. If he uses his money to build a factory, his net worth is likely to decrease. With a reward for hoarding money and a penalty for investing it, the economy may go into a tailspin, a depression that feeds on itself.

Unjust as inflation may be, deflation is worse. The injustice of inflation is somewhat mitigated by the fact that there is likely to be a fairly sizable gross national product to divide; the injustice of deflation is aggravated by the fact that the product to be divided is itself shrinking.

The foregoing generalizations hold when the price level is alternately rising and falling. What happens when the price level continually rises, ratchetting itself ever upward as it has during the postwar years, causing expectations of further inflation? This is another question, one to which experience has not yet given a satisfactory answer.

Much governmental regulation comes from efforts to redress the unfairness caused by price level changes. This can be said of legislation enacted during the Great Depression. If the value of the dollar could be kept relatively stable, the need for government participation in economic life would be much reduced.

If one had to pick out the most useful concept regarding money, credit, and prices, it would probably be what is called the quantity theory. This theory has been both applauded and maligned. It was the dominant explanation for the price level for 150 years prior to the advent of Keynesian economics. It then went into a decline, from which it is now making somewhat of a recovery. What we shall consider here is not the strict, old-fashioned theory with its many unrealistic assumptions; we shall deal rather with the broad idea implicit in the theory, namely, that a large increase in the amount of money is likely to be accompanied by a rise in prices, and that a shrinkage in the volume of currency probably will be accompanied by a price decline.

The quantity theory is often written in this form, called the equation of exchange:

$$MV \equiv PT$$

where:

M = money, the amount of it (usually currency plus demand deposits),

V = velocity, the rate at which money is turned over in a given period,

P = prices, their average level, and

T = trade, the volume thereof.

The equation is true; in fact, it is a tautology. Hence the

three bars rather than an equals sign. All it says, really, is that the money paid for goods equals the money received for goods. The theory is useful. It is clear from the equation that, other things equal, a change in the amount of money will bring about a change in prices in the same direction. It will be properly said, of course, that other things may not hold constant. If the amount of money is increased, the velocity may decrease by a like amount, negating any effect on prices. Or the amount of trade may increase correspondingly, canceling out any change in price. The initiating forces may enter the system through velocity, trade, or prices as well as through the volume of money.

If a regulatory body had enough power over the amount of money and would exercise this power in resolute fashion, considerable discipline over the price level could be achieved. Undoubtedly there would be slippage; velocity might not hold conveniently still so as to give a one-for-one effect of money on prices. Maybe an effort to check a price rise by holding down the supply of money would express itself in an adverse effect on the volume of production and of trade. The relationships are complex, the matter is delicate, and risks are ever present. But the illusion that money is self-regulating has now been left behind (this myth is so outdated and lifeless that it does not even appear in my formal list of myths). The task of regulating the volume of money, and thereby exercising the desired effect on the price level and on trade, has been given by law to the Federal Reserve Board. We shall next see how these delicate maneuvers are carried out. Some descriptive material, however, must first be considered.

I shall not present here the detailed structure of the banking system. This information can be found in a number of standard economics texts. Instead, I shall show that checking accounts, sometimes called demand deposits, constitute the bulk of our money, show how a change in the volume of these checking accounts takes place, and indicate the tools that are available to the Federal Reserve Board for influencing the size of the money supply.

In mid-1966 this was the composition of the nation's money supply:

Coins	$ 4.2 billion
Paper currency	37.9 billion
Checking accounts	133.5 billion
	$175.6 billion

Anyone who has difficulty in thinking of his checking account as money should reflect that he uses his account as if it were a supply of coins or banknotes. In a practical sense it must be so considered.

A key to understanding the size of the money supply is to comprehend how checking accounts, or demand deposits, come to be increased or decreased. Accordingly, a brief excursion into this rather complex subject.

First, it is well to realize that any bank is a business, interested in making a profit. This it tries to do by loaning, at interest, the money deposited with it. It cannot loan out all of the money on deposit; prudence and banking regulations require that a certain amount of its deposits be kept on reserve. This percentage varies. A good round number is 20 percent. Thus, if a bank receives new demand deposits totalling $1,000, it must keep $200 of this in reserve. It can increase its loans by $800.

Consider now a major idea, the idea of multiple expansion and contraction of credit. Suppose our bank, which for the purposes of our illustration we will call a first-cycle bank, receives $1,000 of new deposits. (Later in this chapter we shall consider where these deposits might come from.) It can increase its loans by $800. Let us say that a loan of $800 is made to a building contractor, who deposits the loan in his own bank, a different one, which we will call a second-cycle bank. This bank must also hold a 20 percent reserve, or $160, and can loan out $640. If we keep on in this fashion, after many cycles we find that total loans could increase by about $5 for every $1 increase in the original deposit. "Multiple expansion" is a good term for this process. Conversely, if the first-cycle bank experienced a withdrawal of $1, the total volume of credit might shrink by $5. The ability to add to or to reduce deposits is a powerful tool in monetary policy.

For this system really to expand the amount of money, four things must happen:

(1) Banks must somehow receive new reserves.
(2) Banks must be willing to make loans rather than hold new excess reserves.
(3) Someone must be willing to borrow from the banks.
(4) The public must be willing to leave its money on deposit with the banks, not depleting them of reserves.

Sometimes these conditions do not prevail. In that case, the intention of the Federal Reserve Board to expand or contract credit is for naught or is only partially effective. It is commonly (and properly) believed that the Federal Reserve Board can be more effective in restraining citizens who are anxious to borrow than in persuading an apprehensive public to undertake credit expansion. The apt analogy here is to view the Board as a string-pulling body. "You can't push on a string" expresses the thought very well.

There is another expression that characterizes the general policy of the Federal Reserve Board; it "leans against the wind." If the economic winds are blowing in an inflationary direction, credit is restricted. If the weather is deflationary, the policy is to expand credit.

We now come to the very important question broached a few pages back: What tools does the Federal Reserve Board have to influence the amount of deposits?

Suppose the winds of inflation are blowing and the Board wishes to lean against this wind, reducing the amount of money and credit so as to hold down prices. What can it do? Its most potent tool is to sell some of its government bonds in the financial markets. This is called an open-market operation. The buyer of the bonds will pay the Federal Reserve System with a check, drawn on its bank account. If the Fed (the popular contraction for the Federal Reserve System) sells $1 billion worth of bonds, payment for these bonds will reduce reserves of member banks by $1 billion, and if banks are fully loaned up, will, through multiple contraction, ultimately reduce demand deposits by $5 billion. If the Fed desires to expand credit it buys government bonds, paying member banks in the form of deposits which can serve as a basis for multiple expansion. This buying and selling is the process by which reserves are created or extinguished, the beginning of the process of multiple expansion and contraction referred to earlier.

Another tool is discount-rate policy. The Fed can increase its interest charge on the loans it makes to member banks. The higher rate probably will somewhat reduce the amount of borrowing and the amount of money in circulation. In addition, it will make clear the Fed's appraisal of the economic situation and will set a restrictive tone for the financial markets.

The Federal Reserve System can also change reserve requirements. If it wishes to check the growth in the money supply, it can require the banks to hold larger reserves against their deposits. This tool is powerful and abrupt, infrequently used.

If the Fed's appraisal is that a greater volume of money is needed, then, of course, these actions would be reversed.

How effective are these actions? The tools themselves are fairly potent, though there may be considerable slippage. There will be times when the people are so intent upon borrowing, spending, and investing that restrictive action by the Federal Reserve System only partially checks them. On the other hand, people may be pessimistic about the future; there may be an abundance of reserves lying unused in the banking system. An effort on the part of the Federal Reserve System to stimulate the economy by expanding credit may result in merely increasing the amount of excess reserves lying unused. A price rise might be under way and restrictive action would be effective, but the Board might hesitate to act because of fear that a contraction in credit might set off a business recession. Monetary policy might be partially offset or canceled by unsound taxing and spending programs, which might push the economy in the opposite direction.

But, on the whole, regulatory tools are there, they can be effective, and the disposition to use them is much greater than it was thirty years ago. The Federal Reserve Board will never again forego the full use of its powers in the event of a serious deflation such as occurred during the Great Depression.

It should be emphasized here that the Federal Reserve Board does not have sole responsibility for achieving the desired combination of prices and economic activity. As we saw in Chapter Four, and as we shall see again in Chapter Fifteen, fiscal policy (taxing and spending by the federal government) is the other great tool for achieving stability and growth without inflation.

We have treated our subject up to this point as if the United States were autonomous with respect to its price level, that is, free to determine its policies without reference to other countries. This is not really true so long as we trade with other countries and insist on having a fixed exchange rate between the dollar and other well-established currencies. In Chapter Nine we became familiar with the law of one price, which says that only one price will prevail in a competitive market. In a sense, the world is such a market. Commodities that are generally traded must bear considerable similarity of price, country by country, certain quality differences and transportation costs considered. If prices in the United States were to rise relative to prices in other countries, and if we were to insist on maintaining the exchange value of the dollar, then with our costs high it would be hard for us to export. At the same time, imports would flood into the attractive and high-priced American market. With imports increasing and exports diminishing, we would have to transfer gold overseas, to settle the adverse trade balance. If this were continued, we would have a balance-of-payments problem. The level of prices in other countries would then restrict our capability to establish our own price policies, and would inhibit our free use of fiscal and monetary tools. (It is recognized that balance-of-payments problems have arisen also from other causes: heavy overseas outlay for defense, foreign investment of American capital, a big foreign-aid program, or a net deficit from tourism.)

Of course if we were not concerned about maintaining the exchange value of our currency, we could follow whatever price policy we wished. The dollar would then find its level of value in the foreign exchange markets, equating prices in the United States with prices in the rest of the world. We have learned much about monetary policy, but we have not yet learned how, simultaneously, to pursue our own independent price policy and keep the exchange value of the dollar at a fixed level.

CHAPTER FIFTEEN

The new
economics

Adam Smith and all his kith
Want an unseen hand to guide us,
While Maynard Keynes doth, at some pains,
A steering wheel provide us.

In this chapter we take up what is called "the new economics." The new economics is a body of thought charging government with responsibility for maintaining full employment and specifying the tools, largely supplied by John Maynard Keynes, for achieving that objective. Other names attached to this set of ideas, having somewhat different shades of meaning, are "Keynesian economics" and "macro-economics" (translated: "aggregative economics"). Several features, besides its recent prominence, distinguish the new economics from older forms of the discipline:

First, its concern with aggregate quantities rather than with individual units.

Second, its greater awareness of the important role of expectations in economic life.

Third, and most important, its insistence that the theory it offers is *general,* coupled with its contention that the previous body of theory is concerned with *a special case.*

169

This latter point, a difficult one, calls for elaboration. If it is understood, all that follows is comprehensible; if not, all will remain obscure. In pre-Keynesian economics it was generally assumed that the economy would be at full employment. What this meant, usually, was "substantial full employment," not that every employable man would have a job. In a practical sense, the nation could be at substantial full employment with 4 percent of the labor force unemployed. Some of this group would be "frictionally unemployed," that is, between jobs. Some would be poorly trained and not readily employable. "Full employment" or "substantial full employment" refers not only to labor but to employment of resources generally, including industrial plants. Pre-Keynesians believed there might be some temporary departures from full employment, but these were related to adjustments that were under way; if we departed from full employment, we would rather soon return to it for this was the equilibrium point toward which economic forces were continually driving. Economic analyses generally made these assumptions.

Then came the Great Depression, with one-fourth of the labor force unemployed and industrial production cut almost in half, a dreadful situation that dragged along year after year. The full-employment assumption of pre-Keynesian economics was shaken to its foundations. Economists were without explanation for this catastrophe, and without remedies. How could they interpret a problem which, by their assumptions, could not exist? How could they recommend remedies for it? It was rather like asking a mother to suggest how she might straighten out her delinquent son, whom she thought perfect.

Into this impasse came the new economics. The essential position was that there could be equilibrium when resources were less than fully employed, that under certain conditions

170

the economy could stagnate, continuing indefinitely with a large share of its labor force unemployed and with many of its factories shut down. An explanation was offered which purported to be a *general* theory, applicable in every case, whether the economy was stagnant or whether it was growing. The contention was made that the old body of economic thought was a *special case,* applicable only when resources were at or near full employment. "No quarrel with the old doctrine when the economy is fully employed," said the Keynesians, "but we do differ greatly when there is economic slack. You old boys are right whenever the economy is at full employment. We're right *all* the time."

The new theory is best explained by examining the fundamental ideas in the Keynesian system:

(1) A major driving force for the economy is the level of total spending. Total spending is the measure of aggregate demand. Within limits, the higher the level of spending, the greater will be the total amount of goods and services produced. In Keynesian economics, consumption and demand are central; the older economics focused much more sharply on production and supply.

(2) Spending has three components: spending for consumption, spending for investment, and spending on the part of government. The level of consumption depends in large part on psychological attitudes, which result in a particular propensity to consume. The level of investment depends on profits, expectations, and the rate of interest. The level of government spending is a matter of public policy.

(3) Savings are a key to the system. Income may be spent or it may be saved. The purpose of saving, fundamentally and ultimately, is investment. But saving is done by one set of people, prompted by one set of motives, and investment is undertaken by another group, for related but not identical motives. The two may not agree. If aggregate savings exceed aggregate investment, the level of spending decreases and the economy slows down. If aggregate investment exceeds savings, spending rises and the gross national product increases.

(4) People differ in their saving habits. The poor spend virtually all they receive, sometimes more, and shunt no funds into savings. The wealthy people save a considerable share of their incomes and may withdraw excessive sums from the income stream.

(5) As a result of the forces described above, with a low propensity to consume and a weak inducement to invest, equilibrium can occur with resources less than fully employed. This equilibrium might continue for a long time. In such a situation, government can bring about full employment by either spending more or cutting taxes.

(6) If the economy is fully employed and spending continues to increase, this expenditure will express itself in a price rise. Inflation is not usually a problem when there are unemployed people or factories; inflation is a problem of a fully employed economy.

The logical consequence of this analysis is that if the economy is less than fully employed, government spending

172

should be greater than taxes; the government should then operate in the red. If the economy has been overstimulated so that it is at full employment and spending is excessive, inflation results. Then the appropriate action is to mop up some of the excess income, either by increasing taxes or by reducing the level of government spending.

The new economics looks on taxing and spending not simply as a way of meeting the costs of government, not indeed just as a way of taking the peaks and troughs out of the business cycle, nor just as a way of stabilizing the value of the dollar. It is all of these things plus a way of achieving a high level of economic activity, full employment, and a rapid rate of economic growth. Clearly, the new economics enlarges the role of government in economic affairs.

The new economics is certainly suited to industrialized countries which are experiencing economic stagnation; how much more than this it offers remains to be seen. The less-developed countries that have tried to use it have experienced marked inflation. The "general theory" may not be as general as has been claimed. There may be as great a danger in universalizing the new economics as there was in dogmatizing the old. Doctrinaire economics is dangerous. A "new fogy" may be no better than an "old fogy." The old economics assumed that supply created its own demand, which was an error. The new economics sometimes seems to assume that demand creates its own supply, which is also an error.

The theory is essentially nationalistic and does not satisfactorily take into account international price influences and the discipline of international trade. It assumes that countries can be largely autonomous in economic policy decisions, whereas this is only partially true.

Holding full employment in high esteem as it does, and

stressing deficit spending as a means of achieving this goal, the theory appears to have a built-in inflationary bias. Furthermore, on the basis of experience, it is evident that the inflationary process can occur while the economy is considerably short of full employment. The new economics was developed to overcome a depression, and while its tools might be used in reverse to check an inflation, there has been very little disposition to employ them thus.

Theory assumes that the obstacle to full employment is a lack of consumer spending. Actually, there is the possibility that unemployment may be in part a result of inadequate vocational training, various forms of discrimination, immobility of labor, high wage rates, and administered prices. These obstacles are not readily overcome by deficit spending. Some economists contend that the long-relevant classical theory would still be applicable except for the institutional rigidities which, in the modern society, retard adjustment. They hold that the new economics simply accommodates and institutionalizes the unwillingness of labor and industry to accept downward wage and price adjustments.

Certainly the new economics has attracted some extreme advocates of deficit spending, people who overrate the capabilities of the new techniques and who heavily discount the danger of inflation. Some of the disciples have overstated the master's views, and the master, now twenty years in his grave, is not in good position to refute them. Prior to his death, while traveling through the South, Keynes confided to his companion, Robert B. Anderson, later to be President Eisenhower's Secretary of the Treasury, that his writings had been taken to mean a great many things they didn't really mean and that his ideas were even then changing, with changes in world events.

It is hardly surprising that the new economics is still

somewhat unsettled. No major new economic concept reaches maturity in thirty years. However, with the reservations noted, it is clear that the new thinking has put economics through its most fundamental change in the last hundred years, and that the effects of this change will be felt for many years to come. The likelihood of a protracted depression has been very much reduced by the new economics. This is a tremendous gain. Criticisms should be softened by awareness of this gain.

Milton Friedman says that two authors who are read the least but have influenced mankind the most are Karl Marx and John Maynard Keynes. But here the resemblance ends. In their objectives these two were far apart. Marx sought to do away with the enterprise system; Keynes sought to improve its functioning so that it might survive.

As often is the case when something new appears, there is a tendency to choose up sides between the new and the old. There is now a division between those committed to macro-economics (largely Keynesian, dealing with aggregates) and those committed to micro-economics (largely classical, dealing with individual cases). I believe this quarrel is harmful. Each body of theory needs the other. It is perfectly clear from the history of the 1930's that micro-economics was not in itself sufficient to meet the exigencies of the times. It should be equally clear that the insights provided by Keynes are not themselves sufficient. What is the price level if not an average of individual prices? What is national income if not a summation of individual incomes? What is the level of employment other than the total number of individual jobs? These macro-economic aggregates do not leap into being by magically transcending the individual units of which they are composed. Even if the initiating forces are instituted by a national program, nothing really happens until individual persons managing individual firms make micro-economic decisions. To look at totals without reference to their components is as inadequate as to look at individual units without reference to their sum.

The new economics and the old economics may be closer to a synthesis than is commonly believed. The two are in agreement, as we noted earlier, when the economy is at or approaching full employment. This has been the general situation now for some twenty-five years. Throughout our history as a nation, perhaps three years out of every four could reasonably be counted as years of generally good economic conditions. A pessimistic and, in my judgment, erroneous belief prevailed during the 1930's that stagnation was the expected situation for a developed industrial economy. This, indeed, was one of the myths. Our generally good performance since that time has weakened the myth and made the full-employment assumptions of classical economics more credible.

To the same degree that the new economics makes a depression less likely, it makes more tenable the classical assumption of full employment. In this respect, the two are more compatible than opposed.

In the previous chapter we studied the expansion and contraction of the money supply. In this one we have studied the taxing and spending policies of the federal government. These two tools, both of relatively recent development, have increased our capability for sound economic policy. Intramural battles between rival theoreticians should not blind anyone to the fact that the level of our economic competence has been lifted. The significance of this fact is that, wisely used, these tools can unleash the tremendous drive and creativity of private business firms.

CHAPTER SIXTEEN

Regulation

What shall we say of regulation?
Blessing or abomination?
Bane or boon? It all depends
On what the means and what the ends.

"All this talk about economic principles!" says the student. "All this stuff about market forces and competition! It doesn't mean a thing! The government regulates everything; what room is left for the operation of economic laws? Why study economic principles?"

The government does indeed regulate much of our economic lives. Of total spending in the United States, local, state, and national governments together pay out approximately one dollar in four and regulate the spending of additional sums. That this limits the field within which competitive economic principles are free to function is entirely clear.

However, this is not a valid reason for sidestepping economic study. The competitive system should be studied, whatever one's purpose. It should be studied, obviously, if one wishes to defend it; how support it unless one understands it? It should be studied if one's purpose is to improve its functioning, just as a mechanic would study the carburetor he intends to adjust. Economics should certainly be studied if one is intent upon criticizing the system; how know the points to attack

177

unless one has studied the system's weaknesses? Our economic system should be studied even by those who wish to replace it, for any new system would have to take into account the desires, attitudes, tendencies, and forces that express themselves through our present one. The man who wants to escape the study of economics will need some other excuse than the contention that "the government runs everything."

The scope of governmental regulation is indeed great and growing. In the year 1900, total local, state, and federal expenditures by government equaled about 7 percent of the gross national product. Today, the figure is about 26 percent. This increase is in part a measure of increased regulation, in part a measure of the burden of armament.

We saw in Chapters Fourteen and Fifteen how the government regulates the supply of money. Let us now think of other regulatory actions. The Interstate Commerce Commission regulates railroad rates. The Securities Exchange Commission regulates the stock market, and the Commodity Exchange Authority supervises futures trading on the Board of Trade. To regulate business we have the Sherman Act, the Clayton Act, and the Robinson-Patman Act. Public utilities are regulated. Aviation is regulated by the Civil Aeronautics Board and the Federal Aviation Authority. International trade is regulated through tariffs and quotas, administered by the Treasury Department. Farmers are regulated by the Agricultural Stabilization and Conservation Committees, those who buy livestock are regulated by the Packers and Stockyards Act, and those who retail the meat are regulated by the Federal Trade Commission. The Food and Drug Administration regulates what we eat, truth-in-labeling laws regulate what we wear, and zoning ordinances regulate where we can live. Other economic regulations include minimum wage laws, compulsory workmen's compensation laws, maximum hours laws, laws governing employment practices, and laws governing collective bargaining. During the year 1965, 13,000 bills were offered in the House of Representatives, almost all of them with some economic impact, intended or unintended. Hundreds of these were enacted. Almost no old laws were repealed.

Most people think that regulations, being publicly enacted, protect the public interest from the private interest. This is true only to a degree. What measure of need does the Congress use in determining whether a regulation is to be instituted? Abuse of the general welfare? Poor allocation of resources? The existence of poverty? A level of living below one that formerly existed, below one that is possible, or below one that is hoped for? Or simply the amount of clamor for a regulation? All of these factors are considered, of course. But the last one comes through more clearly than the others. And often it is not the public that clamors for a regulation, but the executive secretary of a special-interest group who first sells the membership on the alleged need for a regulation and then strengthens his position by carrying the banner for it. The wheel that squeaks gets the grease. How else explain industrial tariffs, farm price supports, and much labor law? What we have, often, is a farmer lobby working for a higher price, a labor lobby working for higher wages, and a business lobby working for higher profits. If these lobbying efforts are all successful, they result in the multiplication of mutually offsetting regulations. It may be necessary to maintain a lobby and help write regulations into law, not to gain an advantage, but to keep from experiencing a loss. If other special-interest groups are getting regulations put on the books, even an industry that wishes to be self-reliant may find it needs to sponsor regulations, purely as a matter of self-protection. Competition in the market will then have been replaced by competition in the legislative halls. It is by no means clear that the latter is economically or ethically superior.

The list of regulations may indeed create the illusion that competitive economics has been superseded by government regulation. But, in fact, this has not happened. The popular view is that government regulation cancels economic law. The fact is that government operations, including regulations, must take economic laws into account. These laws can be warped but they cannot be vetoed. The influence of economics on government action is probably greater than the influence of government action on economics. For example, the national government has been trying for thirty years to reduce agricultural production, but it is a debatable point whether total agricultural production is now greater or less than it would have been had government stayed out of the picture. When government considers raising the minimum wage, the level at which the wage can be established is limited by economic law; the nation accepts a certain amount of unemployment in exchange for the higher wage.

The illusion of regulatory omnipotence is heightened by the administrator's technique. His success depends on the credibility of his operation. He does all that he can to see that there is reasonable prospect of success before he moves, and he generally moves so as to experience as little difficulty as possible. By issuing numerous regulations of small consequence, an administrator can create the illusion that he is both active and influential. The public, watching this show, thinks that all power lies with the administrator and that economic forces have been immobilized. Regulations of this type result in only slight deviations from what otherwise would have been. Market forces are masked by bureaucratic maneuvers. The public often is afraid to slough off regulations, not knowing what the market forces might do. In many cases, very little real change would occur. In 1953, President Eisenhower abolished the then-existing price controls despite widespread apprehension that disaster would follow. The price changes that actually came about were minor and in a few months the whole thing was forgotten.

Regulatory activity is of two kinds. One has the intention and often the effect of improving the functioning of the market system. The actions of the Federal Deposit Insurance Corporation are a prime illustration. The insuring of deposits, together with the examination of banks, has improved the banking system and increased public confidence. Bank failures have been reduced, the economy has been stabilized, and the market system functions in an improved manner. There are numerous other successful regulatory ventures that strengthen marketing institutions, improve public acceptance of the competitive system, increase the social dividend, and help preserve a free economy. Among these are the Securities Exchange Commission, which regulates the stock market, and the Commodity Exchange Authority, which supervises trading in futures markets like the Board of Trade.

The other kind of regulation has the intent and often the consequence of eliminating the market and substituting central regulation. An illustration is to be found in laws passed to punish the business community. Some regulatory provisions seem to assume that businessmen are by nature opposed to the public interest. Lowell Mason, a former Federal Trade Commis-

DON PAARLBERG

sioner, stated the matter thus: "As an administrator of two antitrust laws diametrically opposed to each other, it was not difficult for me to accuse everybody at a trade convention with being some kind of a lawbreaker. Either they were all charging everyone the same prices, indicating a violation of the Sherman Act, or they were not charging everyone the same price, a circumstance indicating a violation of the Robinson-Patman Act."

The desire to punish is seldom a useful motive in regulatory action, just as the desire to punish is a poor principle in the upbringing of children. But to correct a flaw takes vastly more wisdom than it does to punish.

Most proponents of regulation will say that the action they propose has as its purpose — its objective, its end — the improvement of the market system. But means and ends tend to be confused. Is improved performance truly the end, and the proposed regulatory action the means to that end, or has the regulation become an end in itself? There is a way to test the motive. Ask whether some other means of achieving the stated end would give equal satisfaction. If the answer is "yes," the purported objective was the true objective and the indicated means was truly a means. If the answer is "no," what was offered as a means was really an end, an objective. As an illustration, a dairymen's organization wants to exclude out-of-state milk from the market; it says its purpose is to safeguard health by keeping out substandard milk. Health is the purported end, a restricted market the alleged means. So we ask the question: Would the dairymen be just as happy if health were assured by inspecting the out-of-state milk? They hesitate and dodge the question. Obviously their real purpose was not to safeguard health, but simply to reduce the supply and thus

182

enhance the price. What they offered as a means to an end was, in fact, an end in itself.

Government regulations may be direct or indirect. Examples of indirect controls are spending, taxing, and credit policies that stabilize the value of the dollar by managing the supply of money. Prices of individual commodities are left free to fluctuate. With the indirect approach economic laws can function with considerable freedom and effectiveness. With direct controls, on the other hand, prices and quantities of individual commodities would be regulated, each by each. Direct controls interfere far more, require far greater intervention, and inhibit the efficient operation of the market.

The form of regulation is important. When socialism was first advocated, a century and a half ago, it meant public ownership of the means of production, that is, land and capital. But in the Western world the movement did not take that direction. Instead of socializing the means of production, most countries adopted regulations that in effect socialized the product. Land and factories were left in private hands; a considerable part of their product was acquired through taxation and redistributed. This method was more acceptable to the people and very likely has been more efficient. However, the process of socialization has gone further than would appear if judged by the original criterion, public ownership of the means of production.

How much government regulation do we have in the United States? How far short of complete regulation are we? There are several rough ways of measuring this. One is to consider governmental expenditures as a percentage of the gross national product. As has been said, this comes out to about 26

183

percent. Another way is to compute the percentage of the working force which is employed in regulatory activity of one kind or another, which turns out to be around 3 percent. To regulate a society completely apparently takes about 10 to 15 percent of the working force. This estimate is based in part on William H. Prescott's study of the Incas in his *History of the Conquest of Peru* (1847). The Incas, who had what was probably the most thoroughly regulated economy in history, required approximately 13 men to regulate 100. Modern military experience appears to confirm this ratio and what we know of Communist nations is not greatly at variance with it. If we accept 10 to 15 percent of the working force as the requirement for complete regulation and compare this with the 3 percent of the United States working force engaged in regulation, we get a ratio of 20 to 30 percent. The same numbers keep coming up. The American economy is perhaps one-fourth regulated and three-fourths free.

Diligence will be required if the free sector is to be preserved or enlarged. World-wide, the drift is toward more and more regulation. This drive comes from the tendency to compare the actual situation with some ideal and from the presumption that government is the proper agent to move us toward the idealized goal. A more sober view would be that the millennium is not for this world, that improvement in the economy's performance is indeed possible and is being achieved through our free institutions, and that the appropriateness — or inappropriateness — of regulation should be considered, case by case. For my part, I would vote for less regulation than we now have.

CHAPTER SEVENTEEN

Economic development

'Twixt nations rich and nations poor
A widening gap doth grow.
A widening gap in a shrinking world
Doth grudge and envy sow.

A "revolution of rising expectations" is occurring throughout the world. In scores of poverty-stricken countries people are becoming aware of the fact that hunger and disease need not be the lot of mankind. They are beginning to believe that things can be better, if not for themselves, then certainly for their children. Not only do they believe that the world can be better, they insist upon action to bring this better world into being.

We in the United States are interested in this revolution. We are interested from the standpoint of compassion; concern for the less fortunate is characteristic of the American people. We are interested in a diplomatic sense; we wish to see the less-developed nations achieve their goals through a free system, compatible with our own. We are interested from a military standpoint; men with empty stomachs do not reason well together. We are concerned with respect to our economic interests; we have come to believe that a country does better in the company of nations that are prospering, just as a person does better if his customers are well-to-do. We are coming to believe

185

that poverty-stricken nations are not good trading partners, just as we have learned that poor neighbors down the block are not good customers at the local stores.

This revolution is certainly in part an economic matter. Whatever useful things the economic discipline has to say on economic development are worthy of inclusion in this brief economic primer.

The usual measure for the level of economic well-being is per capita gross national product, that is, the total value of all goods and services in a given country divided by the population of that country. This measure has important shortcomings in that it does not include those goods and services that are of a subsistence nature and hence do not enter into the exchange economy. Nor does it include any reckoning of nonmonetary satisfactions. Thus, it understates the economic position of the less-developed nations. Nevertheless, it is the best — indeed the only — measure that permits intercountry comparisons. Figures for the various countries are made comparable by converting them to American dollars, taking account of the exchange rate of each country against the dollar. Table XII shows such figures, as compared with data from the United States, for ninety less-developed non-Communist areas for the year 1964, the latest date for which such information is generally available, taken from data supplied by the Agency for International Development. Per capita gross national product in the United States is twenty times as high as the average of the ninety less-developed countries.

The gap between the wealthy and the poor nations is immense. Furthermore, it is widening. While there has been some improvement in the per capita level of economic well-being in most of the less-developed countries during the past twenty years, improvement in the developed nations has been greater.

186

TABLE XII

Gross National Product Per Capita for 90 Less-Developed Non-Communist Areas and for the United States for the Year 1964, Expressed in United States Dollars

	Dollars		Dollars		Dollars
Developed areas	1,950	*Africa (cont.)*		*Near East Total*	265
United States	3,270	Cameroon	125	Cyprus	555
Less-developed		Central African		Greece	584
areas	160	Rep.	90	Iran	220
19 Latin Ameri-		Chad	70	Iraq	255
can Republics	325	Congo		Israel	1,257
Argentina	523	(Brazzaville)	135	Jordan	233
Bolivia	173	Congo		Kuwait	3,225
Brazil	177	(Leopoldville)	80	Lebanon	392
Chile	471	Dahomey	70	Saudi Arabia	190
Colombia	306	Ethiopia	49	Syrian Arab	
Costa Rica	383	Gabon	275	Rep.	155
Dominican Rep.	246	Gambia	85	Turkey	245
Ecuador	215	Ghana	251	United Arab	
El Salvador	285	Guinea	70	Rep.	150
Guatemala	293	Ivory Coast	215	Yemen Arab Rep.	90
Haiti	73	Kenya	88		
Honduras	218	Liberia	175	*South Asia Total*	85
Mexico	454	Libya	365	Afghanistan	85
Nicaragua	325	Malagasy Rep.	95	Ceylon	144
Panama	488	Malawi	39	India	88
Paraguay	208	Mali	65	Nepal	70
Peru	280	Mauritania	138	Pakistan	82
Uruguay	518	Morocco	191		
Venezuela	833	Niger	75	*Far East*	
Other		Nigeria	102	Including Japan	275
British Guiana	291	Rhodesia		Excluding Japan	115
British Honduras	360	(Southern)	224	Burma	67
Jamaica	438	Rwanda	50	Cambodia	132
Surinam	340	Senegal	200	China (Taiwan)	189
Trinidad and		Sierra Leone	115	Hong Kong	392
Tobago	632	Somali Rep.	50	Indonesia	70
Africa		Sudan	102	Korea, South	118
Including		Tanzania	73	Laos	60
S. Africa	145	Togo	90	Malaysia	284
Excluding		Tunisia	176	Philippines	153
S. Africa	115	Uganda	80	Singapore	453
Algeria	225	Upper Volta	45	Thailand	113
Burundi	50	Zambia	167	Vietnam, South	115

Source: Agency for International Development, "Proposed Economic Assistance Programs, Fiscal Year 1967," Summary Presentation to the Congress, Washington, D. C., March 1966, pp. 232–237.

This growing differential is a cause of concern to all, poor and wealthy alike, whether motivated by compassion, enlightened self-interest, apprehension, or envy.

How does economic growth get started in the first place? How does a traditional society break with its past and begin the developmental process? We do not really know, but there is evidence that the answer is only partly economic. Something happens that interrupts tradition — war, drought, pestilence, despotism, forced migration, or exposure to other economies. Innovation becomes necessary. Some innovations succeed. The successful innovations have a demonstration effect. Gradually the idea emerges that things can be different.

In the traditional society life is made tolerable by a low level of expectations. Knowledge that one's lot compares unfavorably with another's increases desire and fuels the drive for achievement. A certain amount of discontent is the driving force that initiates economic progress; there would be none without it. On the other hand, expectations that are excessive relative to existing capabilities produce an explosive situation.

The developmental process is initiated by the desire for change and is fueled by dissatisfaction. As development proceeds, old ways of doing things must be torn down and replaced. This is painful. Those who think that the process of economic development will lead to a stable, placid political and institutional setting are expecting what is quite unlikely to occur.

The tremendous idea that things can be better has now caught hold. The economist, among others, is asked for his insight as to how the developmental process can best be expedited. This is one of the most important questions he can be asked.

Throughout the last half of this book we have encountered a number of key economic principles, not more than a handful:

> The law of demand.
> The law of supply.
> The interaction of demand and supply, determining price.
> The law of one price.
> The principle of diminishing utility.
> The law of diminishing returns.
> The principle of opportunity costs.
> The law of comparative advantage.

These principles have been basic to the economic development of the United States. Through them and in accordance with them our people have saved, invested, modernized, and thus achieved our high level of living. These principles have been sufficiently accommodating to permit us to advance at the pace we chose and to create institutions especially adapted to our circumstances.

Now, as Western economists are asked for their views as to how the less-developed countries might advance themselves, divided counsel is heard. Some would take the American developmental experience as a blueprint and try to fit the less-developed countries into it, a narrow view which overlooks the real differences between America of 1800 and the less-developed world of the late twentieth century.

Others say that differences between the United States and the less-developed countries are so great that the economic principles that were basic to our development are not applicable to the rest of the world. People in the less-developed countries are said to be unresponsive to incentives. The law of comparative advantage is said to be inapplicable. It is said that new economic concepts must be developed, and a number of people are so engaged. But economic principles are rooted in the biology and psychology of human beings. As we are one species throughout the world, so the principles have general application. True, differing levels of education, skill, and institutional development will modify the manner in which these principles operate. But they are relevant. Available evidence so indicates. W. O. Jones of the Food Research Institute at Stanford University reported in 1961 that the economic behavior of primitive tribesmen in Africa was in general accordance with established principles.

Most Western economists, including myself, believe that the basic economic laws are general rather than specific and, therefore, appropriate to international economic development. But we see no reason for rigidity regarding the institutional forms through which these laws operate. A form of land tenure different from our own might appropriately develop. The mix of public and private enterprises might vary from that in the United States. The pace of development might be different. Some of the stages in our development might be telescoped, others leap-frogged, others stretched out. Those committed to the free system, however, believe it is important that there be sufficient regard for the individual so that his freedom advances in step with his capacity for decision-making.

In a free system, development would proceed at approximately the pace desired by the people, generally in the direction they choose. It would be modified by the culture within which it arises and would in turn shape the culture within which it evolves. It might have considerable guidance by government, but if the government were responsive to the people, as is generally true in much of the non-Communist world, then the people's goals would be the major policy determinant.

The key to the developmental process, whatever the system, is the rate of saving and investment. No development occurs so long as the country consumes all it produces; development begins when consumption is foregone and the product saved is invested in capital goods or services or in the education of human beings. Good equipment is so enormously superior, well-educated people are so much more productive, and good institutions so much more efficient that money invested therein pays great returns.

Development is occurring, all over the world, at different rates, from different levels. Ninety less-developed non-Communist areas were listed in the previous table; per capita gross national product is advancing in almost all of them. While far short of hopes, expectations, and promises, this growth is an attainment unmatched in any previous age.

Rivaling the concept of economic development described above is the Marxist doctrine, based on the Communist Manifesto. The economic principles we have studied are in part considered erroneous by the Communists and in part are consciously blocked. In the Marxist view, man is considered to be economically motivated or predominantly so. His major interest is the class struggle, which stems from the exploitation of the workers by the capitalists. History is predictable, producing a sequence of inexorable events. The thinking comes from the philosopher Hegel, accepted by Marx. First there is a thesis, a thing asserted. The thesis helps bring into being an opposed view, an antithesis. These two interact to produce a synthesis, embracing parts of each. The synthesis becomes a new

191

thesis and the cycle is repeated. Thus the change from slavery to feudalism to capitalism, each stage bearing within itself the seeds of its own destruction. Capitalism disappears in a revolution, as the "expropriators are expropriated." For a time, order is provided by the "dictatorship of the proletariat." Finally, the ultimate goal is reached and pure communism emerges in the form of the classless society. At this stage, with the elimination of economic classes, the cause of human dissension is abolished. All then live together in tranquillity, without need for supervision, each producing according to his ability and receiving in accordance with his needs.

I have not felt it necessary to deal with Marxist economics to any appreciable degree in this book, and I offer this brief outline only to demonstrate the fundamental differences between Western economics and the Communist doctrine. And, of course, to point up the divergent choices presently being offered to the less-developed nations.

To aid the cause of economic development, as the Marxists see it, is merely to hasten the inevitable trend toward communism. Obviously they would like to guide this process. Thus they are proponents of economic development and have a foreign aid program of their own.

To the Western economist the Communist view is beset with major errors:

> The labor theory of value, the basis of Communist economic thought, is erroneous, having been rejected by the Western world 150 years ago.
>
> Contrary to Marxian predictions, the change from capitalism to communism, where it has occurred, has not generally come in advanced industrial capitalistic countries from internal revolution. It has come mostly in less-

developed countries, often through the use of military force, frequently applied by an outside power.

There is no evidence that the absence of economic classes would cause people to live together in harmony, without governmental supervision. In fact, most available evidence is to the contrary.

The system is not attractive to people. Where individual people have the opportunity to cross the border between communism and freedom, as in Finland, Berlin, and Hong Kong, they cross in the direction of freedom.

Despite its proven worth, Western economic thought is on the defensive throughout the world. It is being challenged by a resolute and dedicated foe. The confrontation between the free economy and Communist doctrine is perhaps the major issue of this half of the twentieth century.

What are the prospects for the free world? Individual liberty is a powerful idea; what many of the less-developed countries desire comes closer to the American Revolution than to the Communist Revolution. Total output of goods and services in the United States is about twice as great as that of the Soviet Union. The free world outproduces the Communist world by a wide margin and has diversity and maneuverability which its rivals lack. The free economic system draws on the ingenuity and inventiveness of each citizen, while the Communist system is monolithic, relying on the judgment of a few. We have been known to admit our errors and change our course — they are slow to admit errors and even slower to correct them.

Objective appraisal gives the West an immense advantage, which only self-doubt could cancel. What we need above all is to act on the basis of the self-validating belief that a free system is capable of success. We need to build this belief within the United States as well as in the less-developed countries; we shall not present a convincing case for freedom in the world unless our actions are in accord with the principles we profess. The capabilities of a free society are limited only by the beliefs of its citizens. Freedom — world-wide — can succeed if we believe in it, understand what it really is, accept the responsibility to achieve it, and strive to make it a reality for all.

Suggestions for further reading, a short list

I — ECONOMIC MYTHOLOGY

Arnold, T. W., *The Folklore of Capitalism,* Yale University Press, 1937, 400 pages.
Snider, Delbert A., *Economic Myth and Reality,* Prentice-Hall, 1965, 149 pages.

II — BOOKS ON ECONOMICS FOR THE GENERAL PUBLIC

Galbraith, J. K., *The Affluent Society,* Houghton Mifflin Company, 1958, 368 pages.
Hayek, F. A., *The Road to Serfdom,* University of Chicago Press, 1958, 250 pages.
Heilbroner, Robert L., *The Worldly Philosophers,* Simon and Schuster, 1961, 309 pages.

III — COLLEGE TEXTS AND REFERENCES
The General Field

Alchian, A. A., and Allen, W. R., *University Economics,* Wadsworth Publishing Company, Belmont, California, 1964, 924 pages.
Samuelson, Paul A., *Economics,* McGraw-Hill, 1964, 838 pages.

The Competitive Market

Stigler, George, *The Theory of Price,* Macmillan, 1952, 310 pages.
Watson, Donald S., *Price Theory and Its Uses,* Houghton Mifflin Company, 1963, 431 pages.

Monopoly

Bain, J., *Industrial Organization,* John Wiley and Sons, 1959, 643 pages.
Chamberlin, E. H., *The Theory of Monopolistic Competition,* Harvard University Press, 1958, 350 pages.
Fellner, W. J., *Competition Among the Few,* Augustus M. Kelley, New York, 1960, 328 pages.
Robinson, Joan, *The Economics of Imperfect Competition,* Macmillan, London, 1954, 352 pages.

Economics and the Consumer

Hamilton, David, *The Consumer in Our Economy,* Houghton Mifflin Company, 1962, 473 pages.
Mack, Ruth, "Economics of Consumption," *Survey of Con-*

temporary Economics, Bernard F. Haley (Ed.), Blakiston, Philadelphia, for the American Economic Association, 1949–56, Vol. II.

Morgan, J. M., *Consumer Economics,* Prentice-Hall, 1955, 440 pages.

The Economics of Production

Chamberlain, N. W., *The Firm: Micro-Economic Planning and Action,* McGraw-Hill, 1962, 428 pages.

Heady, E. O., *Economics of Agricultural Production and Resource Use,* Prentice-Hall, 1952, 850 pages.

Leftwich, R. H., *The Price System and Resource Allocation,* Holt, Rinehart, and Winston, 1960, 109 pages.

Rewards

Davenport, H. J., *The Economics of Enterprise,* Macmillan, 1925, 544 pages.

Marshall, Alfred, *Principles of Economics,* Eighth Edition, Macmillan, 1948, Book VI.

Miller, Herman P., *Rich Man, Poor Man,* Crowell, 1964, 260 pages.

Money, Credit, and Prices

Bernstein, Peter L., *A Primer on Money, Banking and Gold,* Random House, 1965, 180 pages.

Friedman, Milton, *A Monetary History of the United States, 1867–1960,* National Bureau of Economic Research, 1963, 860 pages.

The New Economics

Hansen, Alvin H., *A Guide to Keynes,* McGraw-Hill, 1953, 237 pages.

Harris, Seymour E., *The New Economics,* D. Dobson, London, 1960, 686 pages.

Wright, David McCord, *The Keynesian System,* The Millar Lectures, Number Four, Fordham University Press, 1961, 90 pages.

Regulation

Bator, Francis M., *The Question of Government Spending,* Harper, 1960, 167 pages.

Fleming, Harold, *Ten Thousand Commandments, A Story of the Anti-Trust Laws,* Prentice-Hall, 1952, 206 pages.

Economic Development

Bauer, P. T., and Yamey, B. S., *The Economics of Under-Developed Countries,* University of Chicago Press, 1957, 271 pages.

Friedman, Milton, *Capitalism and Freedom,* University of Chicago Press, 1962, 202 pages.

Higgins, Benjamin, *Economic Development: Problems, Principles, and Policies,* Yale University Press, 1959, 803 pages.

Knorr, Klaus, and Baumol, W. J. (Eds.), *What Price Economic Growth?,* Prentice-Hall, 1961, 174 pages.

Kuznets, Simon, *Six Lectures on Economic Growth,* Glencoe Illinois Free Press, 1959, 122 pages.

Myrdal, Gunnar, *Rich Lands and Poor: The Road to World Prosperity,* Harper, 1957, 168 pages.
Rostow, W. W., *The Stages of Economic Growth, A Non-Communist Manifesto,* Cambridge (England) University Press, 1960, 178 pages.
Schumpeter, Joseph A., *Capitalism, Socialism and Democracy,* Harper, 1950, 431 pages.

History of Economic Thought

Blaug, M., *Economic Theory in Retrospect,* Richard D. Irwin, 1962, 633 pages.
Lekachman, Robert, *A History of Economic Ideas,* Harper and Row, 1959, 426 pages.

IV — SEMINAL WORKS

Keynes, John Maynard, *The General Theory of Employment, Interest and Money,* Harcourt, Brace and Company, 1935, 403 pages.
Marshall, Alfred, *Principles of Economics,* Eighth Edition, Macmillan, 1948, 871 pages.
Smith, Adam, *Inquiry into the Nature and Causes of the Wealth of Nations,* Vol. II, Second Edition, Oxford, at the Clarendon Press, 1880.

Index

About the
author

Prior to his appointment as Hillenbrand Professor of Agricultural Economics at Purdue University in 1961, Dr. Don Paarlberg was Food for Peace Coordinator and Special Assistant to President Eisenhower. He served eight years in Washington during the Eisenhower administration. For five of these years he was in the Department of Agriculture, where he was assistant to Secretary of Agriculture Benson and then Assistant Secretary of Agriculture, and for three years he was on the White House staff.

He was born June 20, 1911, in Oak Glen, Illinois. In 1940 he received a B.S. from Purdue, in 1942 a Master's from Cornell University, and in 1946 a Ph.D. from Cornell. He began his teaching and research work at Purdue in 1946.

Dr. Paarlberg has traveled in some twenty nations, and has been a consultant abroad for the federal government and for private foundations. His special interests are in the areas of economic development and public policy, and he has written extensively on agricultural subjects. His book, *American Farm Policy,* was published in 1964.

He is married and has two sons, Don, Jr., and Robert Lynn.